Janey Lee Grace

imperfectly
naturalwoman

the pocket book

Crown House Publishing Limited
www.crownhouse.co.uk

First published by
Crown House Publishing Ltd
Crown Buildings, Bancyfelin, Carmarthen, Wales, SA33 5ND, UK
www.crownhouse.co.uk

British Library of Cataloguing-in-Publication Data
A catalogue entry for this book is available from the British Library.

13 digit ISBN 978-184590140-0

Edited by Fiona Spencer Thomas

Printed and bound in the UK by
Athenaeum Press, Gateshead, Tyne & Wear, UK

This book is dedicated to my
family and friends and everyone who has
a vision for a healthier world.

I was gonna take over the world but I got distracted by something shiny.

AUTHOR UNKNOWN

Acknowledgements

After the success of *Imperfectly Natural Woman* it's hard to know where to start saying thanks, but I must credit Caroline Lenton at Crown House Publishing for giving me this opportunity to share my top tips with you. Thanks to Johnnie Walker for giving me the airtime on BBC Radio 2 to argue the 'alternative/holistic' viewpoint which sent the book to Number One on the Amazon Bestseller list overnight, and huge thanks to all of you who have since bought that book or met me at talks and events across the UK. In small ways so many lives have been changed and it's brilliant to hear from you and get your feedback, as well as your own recommendations.

Thanks to my excellent editor Fiona Spencer Thomas, my four beautiful children Sonny, Buddy, Rocky and Lulu and finally, to my wonderful husband Simon – I couldn't have done any of it without you.

Contents

natural alternatives

natural home

Introduction

I hope you'll enjoy this 'pocket' collection of tips and ideas extracted and adapted from *Imperfectly Natural Woman*. This is the perfect pocket book to carry around to remind you that you can indeed have your 'imperfectly natural' cake and eat it.

If the closest you've ever come to natural living is choosing the 'light' version of mayonnaise, this book is for you. If the only recycling you've ever done is chucking your wine bottles into the car park's bottle bank just to rejoice in the crashing sound – it's still for you.

The title is all-important you see. It's 'Imperfectly Natural Woman'. After all, if you were one hundred per cent 'natural' that *wouldn't* be natural. We all have imperfections and we're all at different stages in our life journeys. I believe it is possible to look naturally gorgeous, feel great, do your bit in the green/eco stakes and save cash in the process.

Thanks for buying this book and I hope you'll find it incredibly useful and inspiring. Please pass it on to your friends and spread the word about my free website and e-zines. You'll find the address at the end of the book.

Hopefully, if you take up some of the ideas, you'll be living a little more simply and saving a good few quid into the bargain. You'll be healthier and in a sense, wealthier, and in the currency of doing your bit for the environment, you'll be richer, indeed!

PLEASE NOTE: None of the recommendations in this book is a prescription, more a way to get you thinking about your health and home in a more practical and responsible way – a lifestyle guide.

Its contents are in no way intended as an alternative to professional healthcare and it is advisable to consult your existing healthcare professionals before making any changes to your regime.

All these little ripples of holistic living will some day add up to a sea of health.

JANEY LEE GRACE

natural you

Now I lay me down to sleep,
I pray the Lord my shape to keep.
Please no wrinkles, please no bags,
And please lift my butt, before it sags.
Please no age spots, please no grey,
And as for my belly, please take it away.
Please keep me healthy, please keep me young,
And thank you Dear Lord for all that you've done.

ANON

Save your skin

'Don't put anything on your skin that you wouldn't eat,' say the natural skin gurus.

Mmmm … I'm imperfect, so I probably wouldn't choose to eat the lotions and potions I'm wearing right now but, interestingly, they wouldn't hurt me if I did (and, indeed, the coconut oil would be beneficial – more on that later). When it comes to our favourite skincare products, without wishing to be too scare-mongering, I must tell you a little of what's in them. Most contain ingredients such as artificial colours, dimethicone, ethylhexyl salicylate, disodium EDTA, ethylparaben, methylparaben, propylparaben, preservatives and parfum. Also carcinogenic acrylamide and triethanolamine (an additive in shampoo), which can form cancer-causing oily compounds called nitrosamines.

All the above can cause skin irritation, some have hormone-disrupting potential, alter skin structure and allow chemicals to penetrate the bloodstream and, in the case of the preservatives, have been known to mimic oestrogen and have been linked to breast cancer.

I'm not a scientist but I am aware that, although each of those chemicals will have 'tested safe', it's not possible to test the safety when they interact with each other.

The skin is the largest organ of the human body and, without doubt, what you put on it is absorbed within. After all, that's what the beauty advertisements tell us, so it applies to chemical products as much as it does to harmless food preparations such as coconut oil or avocado face masks.

The positive news is that there is now a huge range of one hundred per cent natural creams, moisturisers and oils available that are every bit as nourishing and pampering as those you may use currently. What is more, they contain NO scary chemicals. There are also lots of 'DIY' recipes when it comes to skincare. So get concocting!

DIY cleansing, toning and face masks

For cleansing oily skin, a very simple foaming cleanser for the face is Liquid Castile soap, made from pure olive oil. Add your own favourite essential oil to give it a lovely smell. (Lemon or lavender work well but don't use lavender if you are pregnant.)

Olive oil cleanser:

In an emergency a tiny amount of olive oil will remove make-up but could be a little too heavy to use every day.

Rose water and witch hazel toner:

You can buy both from any good chemist, or ask them to make up a bottle for you by mixing two parts' rose water to one part witch hazel. It's cheaper and better than any chemical toner you'll find on the market.

Tomato and milk toner:

Even cheaper, use up some of the leftovers in the fridge! For example, you can easily make a home-made cleanser by using tomato and milk. Make tomato juice by straining the pulp and mix it with an equal quantity of milk. Store this in a bottle and refrigerate it for use every day. Spread it on your face and neck with your fingertips; leave it on for ten minutes then wash off with cold water.

Tomato lotion:

Tomato lotion helps shrink the enlarged pores and it can be made by using tomato juice mixed with two or three drops of lime juice. Apply this solution to your face and then wash it off after fifteen minutes.

Tomato face mask:

Tomato pulp tightens skins and is a great remedy for blackheads. For a good complexion, spread the pulp of tomato on your face, leave for an hour, then wash it off with warm water. If done regularly you'll see the results.

Oatmeal and honey facial scrub:

Oats are highly absorbent, hypoallergenic and help to soften skin.

Take a handful of oatmeal and some water and rub over your face for an exfoliating scrub. Or you can make a really simple mask by adding honey. Oatmeal is great for oily skins because it'll absorb excess oil while the honey soothes and smoothes the skin. It's safe for sensitive skins too. Honey is anti-microbial and is also a natural antiseptic. If you like you can also squeeze a capsule of Vitamin B6 into the mixture for even greater benefits.

To make this scrub, throw a handful or so of oatmeal into a mixing bowl and add enough honey to produce a nice thick paste. If you want to use a vitamin capsule, squeeze it in at this stage too. When you have it looking nice and gooey, slap it on your face and leave for fifteen minutes before washing it off with lots of lukewarm water. Then apply your regular moisturiser or facial oil.

Fruit smoothie quick fix for dehydrated skin:

2 teaspoons of oatmeal

2 teaspoons of mashed strawberries

Mix into a paste and massage onto damp skin. Rinse off with warm water.

Actually, any fruit pulp will do (see the section on Juicing). Nothing need go to waste!

Top tip!

Essential oils nourish and moisturise the face.

You might think that if you have greasy skin using oils on the face will make it more so but that's not the case. If you know a good aromatherapist, ask them to recommend some oils for you and, if possible, 'tailor-make' you a face oil. After that you can easily make up your own.

Try to source good quality essential oils (not blends) and you'll need a little dark glass bottle with a dropper.

Facial oil recipe:

To make a good, basic oil (which you can vary each time), you need first to make a base using cold pressed grapeseed oil plus carrot oil. You can add a vitamin E capsule or evening primrose oil and an essential oil.

To a 30ml bottle of this you could add:

eucalyptus 5–10 drops

clary sage 5 drops

thyme linalol 5 drops

lavender 15 drops (avoid in pregnancy)

geranium 5 drops

bergamot 5 drops

Occasionally, you can substitute neroli, fennel, rose or myrrh, depending on how you're feeling.

If you do want to buy a ready-made facial oil blend, you can get excellent face oils from:

www.nealsyardremedies.com

www.greenpeople.co.uk

www.spieziaorganics.com

www.inlight-online.co.uk

www.forestsecretsskincare.com

> ## Emergency handbag kit:
>
> A tiny bottle of pure olive oil ... because it can be used as a make-up remover or a skin moisturiser ... and tea tree oil ... great for wounds, or zits ...

Body beautiful

Scrubs for the face and body

As before, almost any fruit pulp will do the job, mixed with ground almonds, oatmeal or whatever you have to hand. This one smells good enough to eat (and it is!).

Banana scrub:

A yummy scrub for all over dry, sensitive skin.

2 teaspoons rolled oats

2 teaspoons mashed banana

1 teaspoon of honey (Manuka honey is great)

1 teaspoon fresh milk

Mix ingredients, apply all over face or body, then leave for a minute and wash off.

Without doubt, natural oils will moisturise the skin much more efficiently than petrochemical-laden products, so try sweet almond oil, borage and even just extra virgin olive oil, which are both wonderful for skincare. In Europe and Asia, these have been the mainstay of women's skincare and beauty regimes for centuries. But here, if you haven't heard it before, is my top tip for moisturising the body so ditch your expensive lotions and body butters. The cheapest and best moisturiser you'll ever find is coconut oil. (Yes, you can eat it too!)

If possible, source organic virgin coconut oil. It solidifies if left in normal to cold temperatures (65°F) but you simply spoon it out of the jar, rub your hands together and apply it. When it's warmed it turns to liquid so you can smear it all over your body. You'd think it would be greasy or smell of coconuts which, let's face it, is OK if you're on the beach but not ideal all year round. However, incredibly, it has only a faint smell and isn't greasy. Just give it a few minutes to soak in as usual. It's fantastic for pregnancy too, so you can forget all those expensive 'tummy oils'. This is all you'll need.

It's also an incredible hair conditioner, as it softens the hair and conditions the scalp. It's rich in various nice minerals such as calcium, potassium and iron and, if you have dry damaged hair, using the oil as a pre-wash conditioner can revitalise it and rid you of dandruff better than a medicated shampoo.

Lather it on to damp hair, wrap a bath cap and towel around your head and sleep on it, you may need a couple of washes to get it all out the next morning but your hair will be soft and silky.

Coconut oil is wonderful for hands and feet too. If you're not expecting a night of passion, slap it on your feet under thick socks and on your hands under cotton gloves and sleep tight.

My favourite is the ethically traded Coconoil from Sri Lanka www.coconoil.com.

If you want an intoxicating fragrance try Gardenia-scented coconut oil from www.sensitiveskincareco.com.

Bathtime bliss

If I were a psychiatrist, I think I would like to inspect my patients' bathrooms before investigating any other area of their lives.

MARK HAMPTON

If you're a take-a-quick-shower kind of person you may not identify with my wallowing in the bath with a candle and a glass of wine, but nevertheless before you step into the cubicle or lower yourself into the bath, try to get into the habit of dry skin brushing. It really is invigorating and it only takes a couple of minutes. You need to use a natural bristle brush and work upwards from your feet, not forgetting the soles and the backs of your knees. Firm, long strokes are best and you should work towards your heart. You'll tingle at first but you'll soon notice the benefits. For starters, all those dead skin cells will be sloughed away and with them all the nasty toxins. Second, it will help with lymphatic drainage (very important for your immune system, too) and boost your blood flow. You'll feel all warm and invigorated because your circulation has been stimulated.

There must be quite a few things a hot bath won't cure but I don't know many of them.

SYLVIA PLATH

Epsom salts are wonderful to eliminate toxins. Put a cupful into your bath and soak. Dead Sea salt is popular but more expensive than good, old-fashioned Epsom.

For a deluxe treatment, though, it's worth investing in a bag of Himalaya salt. This is lovely and soft and pale pink in colour. It's claimed it can prevent osteoporosis, is a strong natural antihistamine, can benefit the extraction of excess acidity from the cells in the body, in particular the brain cells, and can be beneficial for balancing the blood sugar levels, especially for diabetics. www.amazinghealth.co.uk.

Avoid potentially skin-irritating bubble bath or foam. A drop or two of essential oil will lift your spirits.

Cleopatra style bathing:

For itchy skin, rashes or eczema try the oatmeal bath. Just fill a muslin bag or a thin sock with oatmeal, or porridge oats, tie it at the top and let the water soak through. It feels rather as if you were bathing in milk!

Fizzy bath bomb recipe:

You can make your own bath bomb by mixing 3 tablespoons of bicarbonate of soda with 1 ½ tablespoons of citric acid and a few drops of essential oil. Drizzle a scant teaspoon of water over the ingredients and mix well. This can be used as it is or pressed into a mould and stored in a plastic bag.

If I had a magic wand, I would …

… eat less, exercise more – get a better figure. Lose weight. Love myself more. Stop beating myself up and expecting myself to be a perfect parent. A perfect parent doesn't exist. We just do the best we can with what we have available at the time – and it's usually good enough. Stop worrying about what has been and what might happen tomorrow. Enjoy this moment – that's why we call it the 'present'.

SUE – REFLEXOLOGIST, HOMOEOPATH, MUM OF ONE

Cosmetics

I have girlfriends who look fantastic without makeup – the real outdoor types who look fresh-faced and gorgeous without a scrap of slap. However, I am not blessed with those looks. My features are very undefined and I look like Winnie the Pooh (no offence to Winnie, of course).

Reports have shown that some cosmetics may be loaded with a host of potential carcinogens, neurotoxins and other irritants that can be absorbed through your skin into the bloodstream and end up in your internal organs. Most women absorb around two kilograms of chemicals through cosmetic products every year.

The fantastic news is that since the first print run of *Imperfectly Natural Woman* there are now lots of one hundred per cent natural alternatives to regular cosmetics and you don't need to compromise on quality and luxury.

Look for products claiming to be non-allergenic, composed of inert minerals, environmentally friendly and not tested on animals. Some companies offer organic mineral makeup with a fabulous range of colours, such as Inika www.inikacosmetics.com, Lilly Lolo www.lillylolo.co.uk and Anne Marie Borlind www.annemarieborlind.com.

I don't believe makeup and the right hairstyle alone can make a woman beautiful. The most radiant woman in the room is the one full of life and experience.

SHARON STONE

Easy for her to say!

JANEY LEE GRACE

Sunscreen

The sun has had such a bad press in recent years that most of us now avoid it completely. We plaster ourselves in sun protection factor 30, even under moisturising creams during the winter months, and stay out of the sun. The problem is, when we get one or two weeks' holiday, we go completely mad, forget what we know of the dangers of burning and cook ourselves until we're fully roasted, and basted with a nice chemical concoction.

Some of the ingredients in sunscreen lotions that you might not want to absorb into your skin include dioxybenzone, oxybenzone and PABA (paminobenzoic acid). These chemicals actually inhibit the formation of vitamin D, the one beneficial factor of sunlight. It's thought that around fifteen to twenty minutes daily of 'safe' exposure will provide enough vitamin D for our needs. There's no doubt it makes us feel better, increases our oxygen levels and gives us a great sense of well-being. Remember feeling depressed on those grey winter days, while the first sunshine in spring has us leaping for joy?

The interesting thing we've probably all forgotten is that, many years ago, heliotherapy (exposure to sunlight) was an amazing medicinal tool. That was before there were the many drugs and invasive treatments available now.

Clothes are the safest sun block. I go for the film star image (in my dreams!) and wear a huge sunhat, big sunglasses and pashminas. Silky sarongs and light throws look pretty cool too.

If you use sun creams, make sure they're the more natural ones. Urtekram Sun Lotion factor 24 is a good one. It has to be kept in a cool place when not in use, as it's organic and preservative-free. The ingredients are water, organic apricot kernel oil, plant-based sun block, coconut oil products, peanut butter, vegetable stearic acid … and nothing else! See also www.green-people.co.uk and www.lavera.com.

For the kids, there's a brilliant range of cover-up clothing at www.suntogs.co.uk. If you're concerned about your moles, have a full body screening. www.themoleclinic.co.uk.

Hands and nails

I had little white flecks all over my nails and was advised it can mean a sign of a zinc deficiency. I took 25mg of zinc daily and also upped my B vitamins and calcium.

Silica is also good for nails (and hair), and of course for healthy nails we need essential fatty acids – regular amounts of Omega 3, 6 and 9. I'm fairly sure my nails are stronger for them.

I never use regular soap (far too drying) or conventional hand creams (full of chemicals) because, as with the feet, I just slap on the coconut oil. If I'm sleeping alone I soak my hands first, then lather on the oil and wear protective gloves in bed (surgical ones do the trick). You look a sight but you do wake up with very soft and silky hands.

To replace the oils in nails you won't go far wrong with extra virgin olive oil, but sweet almond oil works just as well and is not as heavy. If you need to exfoliate your hands, use a paste of almond oil or ground almonds and sunflower oil with rock salt, honey and lemon juice.

There are now some more 'natural' nail polishes such as Suncoat, Sante and Nubar, that do not contain formaldehyde and toulene www.guardianecostore. co.uk, Nubar – www.nailz2go.org.uk.

Buffing is great and makes the nails shiny and healthy.

The one thing I couldn't live without …

Music, laughter, lavender oil – oh, that's three!

If I had a magic wand, I would …

… employ a vegetarian chef.

JOSIE –
SINGER SONGWRITER, MUM OF ONE

Natural deodorants

Conventional spray and roll-on deodorants and anti-perspirants serve an interesting purpose as they inhibit one of the body's most natural and important processes, namely sweating. They clog up your pores, are terrible for the environment and they can often cause allergic reactions because they usually contain petroleum, emulsifiers, alcohol, aluminium chloride, propellants and, of course, perfume.

What we often don't realise is that it's not our sweat that smells, it's when bacteria forms that we get whiffy. The whole concept of antiperspirant is a weird one to me. It's hopeless trying to block the pores so that your body can't perspire. That's asking for trouble. It won't destroy the bacteria and the perfume will only mask the odour temporarily.

A natural product such as a crystal deodorant doesn't stop perspiration, therefore it doesn't clog the pores or cover up odours with perfume. What it does is attacks the cause of the problem: the bacteria that cause the odours. When applied, it leaves a fine layer of mineral salts on the skin that can't be felt or seen. The combination of these salts has the unique ability to prevent bacteria growing and, because of the large molecular structure of the crystals, nothing is absorbed into the skin to leave toxic residue or by-products. And there's no smell! It's a revelation for me – another wonder of nature! Crystal deodorants come in the form of a 'stick', like a roll-on, stones, or handy travel sticks.

After a bath or shower, while your skin is still wet, simply apply the deodorant to the areas that need protection and allow to dry. If the body is dry, wet the deodorant with water and use as you would a roll-on, making sure the entire area is covered. Don't leave the deodorant in water, because it will dissolve, but it should last a minimum of six months and probably as long as a year, so it's also very economical.

Top tip!

Crystal deodorants are also great for minor skin complaints and spots! If you get a huge zit on your chin (incredible that it happens even when we've outgrown our teenage angst, isn't it?) just rub the slightly dampened stick gently on the area. It'll go – trust me. And for the boys, it's great when they've slashed themselves during the morning shave, so there's no need for that attractive patch of loo paper! My favourite brands are Pitrok (www.pitrok.co.uk) or the Natural Crystal from Faith in Nature (www.faithinnature.co.uk). They vary in price from around £3 to £8. If you want a natural deodorant but like the idea of a roll-on, try Weleda (www.weleda.co.uk).

Staying young

I can't advise on the menopause yet, as I'm not quite there, though I hope I'll cope naturally, and I won't touch HRT with a bargepole. Wonderful at any time though is the Hormone Replacement Therapy Cake – yes, a cake that's hormone balancing (www.annie-bakes.com). Here's the recipe:

Grease and line two 1lb loaf tins.

Preheat oven to 190°C.

Put all the following dry ingredients into a large bowl and mix thoroughly:

4oz soya flour	4oz wholewheat flour
4oz porridge oats	4oz linseeds
2oz sesame seeds	2oz flaked almonds

2 pieces stem ginger, finely chopped

7oz raisins

½ a teaspoon each of nutmeg, cinnamon and ground ginger

Add

1pt 7fl.oz soya milk

1 tablespoon malt extract

Mix well and leave to stand for 30 minutes

Spoon into tin and bake for about 1 hour 15 minutes until cooked through.

Test with skewer.

Turn out on to rack to cool.

Serve sliced and spread with soya spread or butter. Divine!

Guilty secrets and imperfections

Using Mr Mash instead of making real mashed potato – despite all the other organic, healthy food!

If I had a magic wand, I would …

Spend more time on myself, and get to bed earlier.

JUNE –

HOME EDUCATING MUM OF FOUR

Natural hair care

It won't be news to you to hear that your hair will be healthy if *you* are healthy. It's our 'crowning glory' and for many of us a 'bad hair day' means simply a bad day.

As we get older, our hair tends to become thinner and seems much drier, as the oil glands have slowed down. It also loses much of its colour intensity, even if we haven't actually gone grey. This is because the pigment fades and we produce less melanin.

We need a diet rich in essential fatty acids and certain vitamins and minerals. 'Magic foods' can protect hair from age-related changes. They include liver, a rich source of vitamin A, which is essential for the proper functioning of the scalp's sebaceous glands, and black molasses (the sun-sulphured variety), which can be added to a bowl of yoghurt or taken on its own every day. It contains two milligrams of iron, lots of calcium and magnesium, and is also chock-full of many B vitamins, including pantothenic acid.

Sea vegetables and seaweed of all varieties are the single most potent strengtheners of hair (and, incidentally, nails) you can find in nature. They are a veritable treasure house of essential minerals, including organic iodine, as well as the B vitamins and vitamins D, E and K.

You can buy many kinds of dried seaweed to use in vegetable dishes, soups and curries or, as an alternative, take kelp tablets with every meal.

Here are some common sense tips when it comes to hair care:

- don't wash your hair too often;
- avoid harsh shampoos and conditioners;
- always make the final rinse in cold water to 'close pores' and make the cuticle lie flat;
- never rub or wring wet hair just pat it dry and wrap it in a towel;
- use a natural bristle brush and keep your brushes and combs clean by removing hairs from them and washing them in water and a bit of bicarbonate of soda;
- leave hair to dry naturally whenever you can and avoid using hair straighteners, heated brushes and rollers too often;

- if your hair is looking the worse for wear, have a look at your diet and ensure you are getting the essential nutrients you need.

Dandruff and flaky scalp treatments:

Massage fresh apple or grapefruit juice into the scalp, rinse with a few teaspoons of cider vinegar and water.

Revitalising hair treatment:

Use three parts jojoba to two parts wheatgerm oil to make a base. Add a few drops of essential oils – tea tree, lavender and geranium work well. Apply it to dampened hair and leave on for about half an hour. Rinse off.

If I had a magic wand, I would ...

Mmm, do so many things differently! From studying much harder when I was younger, doing art instead of the subjects I was told to take, to not falling off a motorbike and breaking my bones. We all make mistakes, so trying to learn by them and live with them, without beating ourselves up, is the key.

AMANDA – FOUNDER OF
SENSITIVE SKINCARE COMPANY

Don't wash!

Hair is clever stuff, even self-cleansing, if you let it. I once had a friend who didn't wash his hair for two months and, instead of looking like a drowned rat, he sported the most luscious mop I've ever run my fingers through! Now it's tricky to do that living in the city, with fumes and grime everywhere but it proves that your hair does have a natural balance that can be easily destroyed with sustained heavy-duty chemical intervention. I can't go that route myself, since I can't stand the itching until it finds its equilibrium – but go easy, and go natural.

Shampoos and conditioners

The average bottle of shampoo and conditioner contains a hair-damaging – certainly hair-raising – number of chemicals and toxins. At the very least, if you wash your hair every day with these shampoos, you will be stripping your hair and skin of essential oils and creating a potential skin irritation on your hairline and face.

Choose a natural shampoo containing no parabens or sodium laurel sulphate (or any other nasties found in most of them). Essential Care brought us the first Soil Association accredited organic shampoo, www.essentialcare.com, but I also like ranges from Weleda, www.weleda.co.uk, Green People, www.greenpeople.com, and Neal's Yard remedies, www.nealsyardremedies.com.

The other really fab way to wash your hair naturally and ethically is to use soapnuts. You can make an infusion by boiling six or seven shells in a saucepan, strain off the liquid to make a fantastic shampoo that leaves your hair really soft and silky and protects against head lice. Soapnuts are one hundred per cent natural, so are great for anyone with allergies, and totally environmentally friendly. They are also very economical at around £3 for 100g. See 'Those washday blues' for more information on soapnuts (yes, they wash your clothes too!).

Life is an endless struggle full of frustrations and challenge but, eventually, you find a hair stylist you like.

ANON

Hair to dye for

Are you one of the few women who has never coloured her hair? Oh, how I bow to your good sense! That's the stuff we should be taught in school.

Once you start down that slippery slope you'll be forever at the hairdresser's shelling out hard-earned cash to pile those chemicals into your hair to keep up what you've started. If only I had known back then how cool it would be to stand out for having natural hair in great condition – there would have been no messing.

Many hair dyes and colourants contain phenylene-diamines, ammonia, naphthol, chlorides, propylene lycol, solvents, isopropyl alcohol – the list of synthetic chemicals is endless. No wonder some manufacturers cover themselves by printing a warning on their product labels, alerting people to the presence of these ingredients.

Is there an alternative?

It's easier of course if your hair is in the red spectrum. Henna is a wonderful natural product that works brilliantly but for the rest of us nothing really 'falls off a tree'. Damage limitation is the answer and if you're close enough to Hertfordshire, Daniel Field is the pioneer of organic and mineral hairdressing with plant-based colours. He uses hair colours that contain safer and gentler alternatives to the usual chemical concoctions on offer. They are also recommended by oncologists as being safe for use by chemotherapy patients. He also offers 'Water Colours' for covering grey hair, described as 'the world's first non-peroxide, non ammonia, semi, demi or permanent hair colour'. Daniel Field – 0208 441 2224.

For home colouring, try to buy gentler, plant-based dyes and tints. Leave the maximum amount of time between applications and leave the colour on for the minimum time. There are companies now that offer herbal and plant-based hair colours. No brand of hair dye is risk-free but, whether at home or in the salon, you'll need to test for allergies and choose a 'less chemical' alternative. The leading brand of gentle home hair dyes is Naturtint. Nature's Dream offers guidance and advice on 0845 601 8129 www.natures dream.co.uk.

Top tips!

Always do a skin patch test first.

Try highlighting, or touch up roots, rather than full head colour applications.

There are more PPDs (p-phenylenediamines) in darker shades, so try going one shade lighter.

Drink lots of water to flush through toxins.

Teeth

Most health food shops stock a good range of natural toothpastes.

My favourite is Sarakan, which the kids love too. Weleda also do a good range of natural toothpastes and Green People have a good one for babies.

Toothpaste recipe:

Mix ¾ cup baking soda with ¼ cup of sea salt, add 2 teaspoons of glycerine and enough water to make a paste. After brushing, rinse well and gargle. It's cheap, effective and healthy.

Mouthwash recipe:

The simplest mouthwash is a couple of drops of peppermint or sage tincture in a cup of water. If you've got mouth ulcers, a great mouthwash to use is essential oil of myrrh (yes, of Wise Men fame) in water.

If you want to buy mouthwash, a fabulous natural one is the Neem mouthwash from Junglesale, www.junglesale.com.

Eyesight

The spiritual eyesight improves as the physical eyesight declines.

PLATO

If you're unlucky enough to be as poor-sighted as I am, check out the Bates Method, *The Bates Method for Better Eyesight Without Glasses* by William H. Bates MD (Owl Books).

The Bates Method works on the assumption that the eyes have muscles that move them in different directions and, like any other muscles in our bodies, they need exercising regularly. Looking straight ahead, reading small print, and staring at a computer screen just won't do it.

Bates developed a series of exercises that include looking straight ahead, moving your eyes up and down, side to side, diagonally and so on. Each step needs to be performed five times. Many people do similar exercises to relieve eyestrain after working at a computer screen but Bates also includes some more unusual ones, such as 'palming' – placing your palms over your eyes for a few moments then looking directly at a candle or bright light (and repeating). There's also 'swinging' (not to be confused with any dodgy partner swapping!). This involves standing with feet about fifteen inches apart, staring straight ahead and then swinging from side to side – transferring the weight from one foot to the other.

The other 'natural eyesight aid' is Pinhole glasses. You may have seen these in healthfood shops or in mail order catalogues. They're basically plastic specs with lenses that look completely opaque but are actually covered in tiny pinholes. Wearing them (indoors, obviously, because they do look bizarre!) for a short time each day, perhaps to read, is said to help greatly with 'training' the muscles of the eyes and helping with focus and concentration. They're around £30. (See www.trayner.co.uk.)

If, like me, you're blessed with having to wear glasses and contact lenses, leave them off when you can, or your eyes will weaken over time as they become dependent on the lenses.

To end on an up note, glasses can look pretty cool. Just make sure you get ones that suit your face, which is a science in itself. Anastasia or Buddy Holly never had a problem.

Fitness

When it comes to exercise, I must confess I am excessively imperfect and I do very little to keep fit. My excuse for this major imperfection is that I have four young children (a fitness regime in itself, you might think), a job (well, several jobs) and, with the best will in the world, I simply don't have time.

Since writing the first book, I have started doing yoga twice weekly and I believe it offers incredible health benefits. It helps with breathing, balance, posture, stamina and of course stress levels. It may not help with aerobic fitness though, unless it's Astanga yoga.

Undoubtedly, aerobic exercise makes us feel and look better. When I took up running three or four times a week I felt lean, my skin glowed and I had loads more energy. To be honest, 'running' may be too impressive a term for what I did. I think the official term is 'fartleking' (yes, you read it right!). 'Fartlek' is a Swedish word meaning 'speed-play'. Another term is 'interval training'. It means you run for a couple of minutes, then walk for a couple, building up your time gradually. For me, it was better than starting off fast and collapsing in a heap before I'd even reached the park gates at the end of my road.

Top tip!

Bounce back into shape! Here's one aerobic activity that will do the lot in one. There's no downside, apart from the minimal one-off cost of the equipment. There's no aerobic exercise (well, not that you can do alone) that's more fun than rebounding. Yes, you can literally bounce into shape.

Rebounders (mini-trampolines) are great fun, safe for all ages, even children or elderly people; in fact no one can resist the urge to bounce. Athletes who have injuries or need rehabilitation use them too. You can just bounce up and down, skip, run on the spot, fling your arms around and do lots of 'routines'. The wonderful bit is that you can wear what you like and bounce whenever you like. Watch the TV, listen to music or order the kids to tidy up the playroom. When I got it I knew that keeping fit could be fun. It's impossible not to smile while you're bouncing – ask Tigger!

From a physiological perspective, rebounding will strengthen your heart and lungs (as long as you get a little bit out of breath) and firm up your muscles because of the unique ways in which your body responds to the force of gravity. It's the only complete vertical exercise where all the organs and even the lymphatic system are affected. This is because the action of bouncing up and down, acceleration and deceleration, brings about continual changes in the forces of gravity on your body. It stimulates and invigorates every individual cell, which can help with detoxification and result in healthier skin, higher energy levels and toned-up muscles. When you bounce on a rebounder, your entire body (internal organs, bones, connective tissue and skin) becomes stronger, more flexible and healthier. Both blood circulation and lymphatic drainage are vastly improved. Sounds like magic? Well it is, kind of. You'll feel fantastic with just ten minutes a day. Can't be bad.

> *Dancing is silent poetry.*
>
> SIMONIDES

Check out sports shops and websites for rebounders, but make sure you get a good quality one. All those years back I bought the PT Rebounder and, believe it or not, it's still going strong (www.wholisticresearch.com).

You can get the Probounce from www.juicemaster.com.

Blessed are the flexible for they shall not be bent out of shape.

ANON

Soul searching

As many self-help books will tell you, lots of us are uneasy and dissatisfied with our lot, but, when asked what we want, we have no idea. You've probably heard the saying that many of us spend our lives striving to reach the top of the ladder only to find that, when (if) we do, the ladder was pitched against the wrong wall. I reckon that if you set clear goals and do what's necessary, you'll probably only just fall short of them. In other words, set a list of eight goals and you will probably achieve five or six. It's OK to 'dream a little' and not restrict yourself. You should list your aims and you must state them in the present tense – 'I am successful' etc – as if it had already happened. That's very important for the unconscious mind, which doesn't differentiate between real and imaginary.

> *Dance as though no one is watching you.*
> *Love as though you have never been hurt before.*
> *Sing as though no one can hear you.*
> *Live as though heaven is on earth.*
>
> SOUZA

The best advice I ever had was to make my list of seven or eight 'dreams' and then write a supporting page stating what I could do to make them happen. I didn't read it out loud but I did look at the list most days, and I did try to put some of the intermediate steps in place. Some years after I'd done this exercise for the first time I came across an old notebook and was fascinated when a tatty bit of paper flew out and I saw it contained the first list of goals I'd ever written. Each of the seven things on that list had happened. Why? Because I really wanted them. I do believe that if I hadn't put some time into correctly identifying what I wanted, they might never have happened.

Goal setting and affirming what you really want is something you can easily do for yourself but it can also play a part in counselling or therapy. Hypnotherapists, for example, will often use visualisation techniques.

The power of the mind is incredible. I used the 'writing it down and believing it' technique to get the birth I wanted for my second son (a water birth). I'd already had one very long, difficult labour, so what I wanted might not have been a natural option for me, but I made it happen. I was absolutely determined.

A girlfriend also had an amazing experience with this simple technique. She was a widow and felt ready to meet another partner. Her hypnotherapist asked her to describe the man she wanted. Of course, she said the usual: 'Oh, handsome, rich, kind.' She was advised to be specific. She thought carefully then she wrote her wish list. A few weeks later, two separate friends on different sides of the world rang her to say it had been on their mind that she must be introduced to a friend or colleague of theirs. (They were talking about the same guy!) An introduction was arranged and one year on they were married. Her new partner fulfilled, to the letter, everything she'd listed in detail.

There are no short cuts to any place worth going.

ANON

'Wow!' you're thinking. 'That's it? I just need to write down, "I am a gorgeous film star and married to Brad Pitt" and it will happen?' Now don't get silly! You can daydream but your goals must be grounded in reality. It's unlikely you'll make it as an Olympic swimmer if you don't like getting wet.

If you want to seek professional help, try to ascertain whether you need a psychotherapist, counsellor or hypnotherapist. Or, if you don't suspect deep-rooted emotional issues, you could use a life coach to help you cultivate a positive approach and a strategy to get the best out of your relationships, work or personal life.

Don't forget that friends are worth their weight in gold when it comes to sharing a problem.

Some great, now deemed classic, books on visualisation and helping you set your goals and achieve your dreams include:

Feel the Fear and Do It Anyway by Susan Jeffers (Arrow); *The 7 Ahas of Highly Enlightened Souls: How to Free Yourself from All Forms of Stress* by Mike George (O Books); *The Seven Spiritual Laws of Success* by Deepak Chopra (Bantam); and, mixing psychotherapy with spirituality, *The Road Less Travelled* by Scott Peck (Arrow).

If you'd like a bit of daily inspiration and support from a liberally Christian point of view, look at www.vurch. com. For more 'alternative' Christian ideas and support, try www.moot.uk.net.

Ask and it shall be given to you; seek and ye shall find; knock and it shall be opened unto you.

MATTHEW 7:7

natural alternatives

> *To eat is a necessity, but to eat intelligently is an art.*
>
> La Rochefoucauld

Let food be your medicine

Most of us know that to a certain extent we can control our health and well-being through diet. True enough, I break many of my own ideals but in a perfect world I would …

Never eat processed foods

I believe that processed foods should carry a government health warning, in the way that cigarettes do. It's not rocket science to know that a TV dinner won't be as nutritious as Mum's home cooking. The really worrying bit is the harm it could be doing to us.

There have been several studies proving that in wartime Britain the average person had a healthier diet than we do today. This may seem incredible, because people were certainly not eating 'superfoods', and they'd never come close to a millet-and-quinoa pilaff, avocado-and-grapefruit salad or tofu-and-sprouted-seeds beany burger. Food was rationed and, yes, that's the key. Most people ate less and exercised more (not in the gym but cycling, walking, gardening and just working hard). People grew their own vegetables organically (even though they didn't think of it that way – it was just that there simply weren't many pesticides and chemicals available), baked their own bread or bought it at the local bakery. It would usually have been wholemeal and would contain no chemical preservatives.

Each person's ration book allowed only limited amounts of tea, coffee, sugar, butter, dairy produce and eggs per week, so no one had the opportunity to be overloaded and, apart from the odd tin of corned beef and box of powdered egg, there was very little in the way of heavily processed food. Certainly, no one arrived home from a hard day at work to a microwaved ready meal. In a funny kind of way, our parents and grandparents were living organically and holistically without having to think about it. That was just the normal way of life.

It's easy to get into the habit of cooking from scratch. It really doesn't take very much longer. You can be clever about it and make huge casseroles, soups and stews that you can span over a few days or freeze for when you've less time to cook.

Go organic

Its official: organic foods, particularly fruit and veg, do taste better than their non-organic counterparts. The mass production, the chemicals, pesticides, the long storage and the sci-fi processes used to prolong the fruit's life have all contributed to a deadening of its very life essence. Most fruit and veg have less vitamin and mineral content and contain more environmental toxins and pollutants than fifty years ago.

What about the various organic certifications? I always look for the Soil Association organic accreditation. It is the most widely recognised body and insists on far more stringent testing than some of the other organisations.

Wherever possible, source your organic fruit and veg locally. It's not only the way a plant has been grown that affects its nutritional value but how long and where it has been stored. I'd always recommend growing your own, even if it's only a few herbs and potatoes. If you want to cheat a bit, buy an instant organic vegetable 'garden' from www.rocketgardens.co.uk – tiny, already established, organic plants that can go straight into the soil so, within a couple of weeks, you'll be picking and eating your own produce. If you don't have a garden, they offer herb 'gardens' and kitchen 'gardens' too. Failing that, find a good local organic supplier or opt for a veg box delivery scheme. Riverford Organics are great. They grow most of the food they sell on their own farm at Buckfastleigh in Devon (0845 6002311) and distribute it throughout the UK. Their food can be delivered locally to most areas and you can order from their huge list of produce or just take pot luck with a weekly organic vegetable box.

Let thy food be thy medicine and thy medicine be thy food.

HIPPOCRATES

The great thing about organic box schemes is that you eat what you're given. It's a great way to get out of your usual pattern and into a more natural, seasonal approach to eating by trying different fruits and vegetables. My medium-sized box for the last week in October included potatoes, carrots, onions, cauliflower, Crown Prince squash, a gourmet bag (salad leaves), green and red curly kale, leeks, celery, Brussels sprouts and tomatoes.

(Go to www.riverford.co.uk to find your nearest distributor.)

For other full ranges of organic fruit, veg and general supplies, see www.theorganicfarmersmarket.co.uk.

If you can get together and form a little cooperative with friends or neighbours, you can save a lot of money by buying wholesale. Try www.infinityfoods.co.uk or www.suma.coop.

If you eat dairy, eggs and meat, make it organic, but perhaps eat less for affordability. Seek out sustainable fish and get to know your local organic butcher and fishmonger, if you're lucky enough to have one.

If I had a magic wand, I would …

… leave for a faraway place for a few months to do yoga and eat simply.

SIMON – DAD OF ONE, PROPRIETOR
OF MAKING WAVES HOTEL

Raw energy

Raw food is packed full of vitamins, minerals and enzymes. It's a shame many of these nutrients are destroyed in the cooking process. A raw food diet is one of my big recommendations for slimming, energy, detoxing, increasing your vitality and protecting yourself against disease. At least consider having a good percentage of your food raw.

If I had a magic wand, I would …

There are no magic wands … understand that each day is a new one and you can make it new all over every morning, if you want to. Attitude is everything. Like the song 'Live like you are dying'. Easy to say, hard to do but good to remember when things are tough.

JANICE — MUM OF THREE

The cooking process

If you're imperfect like me and find it difficult to keep it up, the answer could be to get as close as you can to raw. Try a raw-ish 'stir fry veg' using the tiniest amount, say a teaspoon, of olive oil. Let it get hot but not smoky and then chuck in the veg. The plan is just to 'sear' the outside and keep the vegetable inside crisp, light and raw. It's the best of both worlds. A dash of tamari near the end of cooking is great but, even better; add balsamic vinegar and lemon juice.

Steaming is much better than boiling for 'light' veg. Try an old-fashioned steamer basket, an on-the-hob style steamer or an electric one.

Take a look at your cooking equipment too. Those very efficient non-stick pans could be doing you serious harm. Some non-stick coatings are made with a complex mixture of perfluorinated compounds (PFCs). It's widely accepted that PFCs can be dangerous. They don't biodegrade and the toxins accumulate in people, animals and the environment. It's difficult to avoid

PFCs completely, as they're in electrical goods, furniture, some clothing and rainwear, car engine parts – in fact just about everything man-made! But at least try not to cook with it too often. Replace your non-stick coated cookware with stainless steel or enamel-coated cookware. I've just invested in some heavy but fantastic cast iron pans. For baking or cooking pizzas, meat and fish I use the amazing stoneware plates from Pampered Chef www.pamperedchef.com.

I never use a microwave oven. Putting high-energy microwaves into food disrupts its cellular and molecular structure, and it's hard to quantify exactly the effect that has on the vital force of our foods.

> *When diet is wrong medicine is of no use. When diet is correct medicine is of no need.*
>
> ANCIENT AYURVEDIC PROVERB

Barbecues and smoked food

Of course, we all love a barbecue; it's fantastic to eat outdoors and enjoy that wonderful smell of hickory chips and charcoal. But beware of too much meat and fish cooked on the 'barbie'. There are hydrocarbons in the smoke that can disrupt the fat and protein structure in foods. This can create free radicals (yes, the nasty carcinogenic kind), which some say can contribute to tumours in the body. Scary stuff. Don't go completely mad and vow never to have an outdoor cook-up again, but do take these precautions: marinate the food really well before cooking; be patient and wait until the embers are grey; don't ever cook while the charcoal's flaring up.

Alcoholic beverages

Of course, if you're imperfect like me, you will want a tipple now and again but it scared me when I first realised the hair-raising number of chemicals usually present in the average bottle of wine. The really annoying thing is that currently there is no legislation making it compulsory to list ingredients on drinks, so most wine labels will tell you where the grapes are grown, and that's about it. Vegetarians should be careful, too, because often the ingredients include, or certainly the process has involved, the use of animal products.

All is not lost though. There is an increasingly wide range of excellent organic wines and they're becoming much more affordable. Ask your local off-licence to get some for you, or buy them by mail order from The Organic Wine Co Ltd (01494 446557) or Vintage Roots, who also sell organic spirits (0800 980 4992; www.vintageroots.co.uk). For organic beer, try Black Isle (01463 811871; www.blackislebrewery.com) or you can try www.alcoholfree.co.uk.

Coffee

When it comes to coffee, much as I love it, it's just not great for you. Most of us will consume about thirty-two gallons a year. With non-organic beans, that means about eleven pounds of fertilisers and eight ounces of pesticides will have been used to 'mash up' our annual brew. Scary chemicals such as benomyl, chlordane, carbofuran, DDT, endulfan, paraquat and zineb could all have been used in the production process, though some are banned in certain countries. I prefer my coffee without, so I go organic and fair trade. An easily available one that I like is Percol Organic Americana

– fair trade of course. (See www.coffee.uk.com.) By the way, don't even consider decaffeinated: the process often causes worse effects than caffeine.

Teas

Green tea contains many anti-oxidants including polyphenols which are bioflavanoids that act as super anti-oxidants. It does however still contain caffeine, although only about one fifth of that of normal tea. To be absolutely honest, I'm imperfect on this one. I just hate the taste. If you can drink it regularly, go for it!

There are lots of excellent organic herbal teas and it really just depends on your taste, unless you're using them therapeutically (peppermint is great for digestive problems; chamomile is good for stress and insomnia).

Clipper Teas do a brilliant range of organic teas. The packaging is made from one hundred per cent biodegradable, non-chlorine-bleached material from managed sustainable forests, and they use only unbleached tea bag paper. They also do a sensational hot chocolate. (See www.clipper-teas.com.)

My top parenting tips:

Follow your instincts and learn to trust them. Enjoy your children as much as you can – they will be the fastest-growing things you have ever known. When you have a frazzled moment, stop, sit down and do a group hug.

I'd also like to recommend ...

as much fresh air as you can get.

LIZ – MUM OF THREE, FOUNDER OF
TEAM LOLLIPOP (CLOTH NAPPIES)

Juicing

There are loads of great books on the benefits of juicing. It's the fast-track way to get your (at least) five portions of fruit and veg every day. It can be totally creative – you can combine just about any fruit, seed or vegetable you choose. Drinking fresh fruit and vegetable juice is the quickest way to absorb easily all the nutrients, phytochemicals and enzymes found in plant food that we need to make us healthy. They are cleansing and give us energy.

Celery juice is said to help asthma and bronchitis and to lower blood pressure; radish juice controls coughs, soothes sore throats and reduces fever; and pineapple juice aids digestion and cardiovascular disease. Carrot is a bit of a wonder food and fantastic to juice up on its own or mix with other things. As well as being a great source of beta-carotene and vitamin A, new studies have shown that carrots contain falcarinol, a substance that can help prevent the development of cancerous tumours.

My absolute favourite pick-me-up, though, is carrot, beetroot, a chunk of lemon including the peel and a few scrapings of fresh ginger. (Top tip – always keep ginger in the freezer, and grate it like Parmesan.)

You can also, of course, try the trendy wheatgrass juice, which is all the rage in juice bars across the States. It's one of the richest sources of chlorophyll you can get. It's said to boost your immune system and protect against colds and infections. You can grow it and juice it yourself but you may want to gen up a bit from a book and perhaps buy an automatic sprouter (more about sprouting and relevant equipment later).

The truth is that juicing is time-consuming. Buying the fruit and veg, chopping and slicing it, disposing of the waste (into the compost, I hope), cleaning the chopping board and knives and, worst of all, dismantling the juicer to clean all the individual components, is a long process. Buy a wide chute juicer, especially if you want your children to be able to make their own fresh juices, as there's very little chopping needed and they take apples etc. whole.

Get lots and lots of your favourite fruits and vegetables and leave them next to the juicer in a huge wooden bowl. It's also a good idea to keep a wooden chopping board and a decent knife handy, so the whole ensemble will look you in the eye as you walk past and, if it could talk, it would say, 'Well, lazybones, gonna get a power-packed glass of live enzymes straight into your gut – or what?'

Finally, when you've made your morning juice (or a big flask to keep in the fridge and drink later), clean your juicer straightaway. There's nothing more depressing than getting up the next morning raring to whizz up a healthy spirulina juice and finding it full of rotting fruit dregs. Just do it immediately and – another top tip – keep a nailbrush handy to dig out those awkward bits. Another wondrous tip is that the fruit and veg pulp can be used for a truly natural face pack!

Don't forget you can add seeds, flax oil, yoghurt and protein powders to smoothies and juices.

There are loads of books on the benefits of juicing and some innovative recipes. Get any of the excellent books by Jason Vale, the Juice Master, such as *Turbocharge Your Life in 14 Days* (Thorsons). www.juice master.com.

Old-fashioned homemade drinks

If you can't face juicing, here are a couple of recipes for old-fashioned homemade drinks. They're delicious, healthy, require no special equipment, kids love them and you get the added bonus of sneaking in immune-boosting vitamins without them knowing!

Lemon Barley Water:

Put 100g of pearl barley (it's labelled as pot barley in some health food shops) into a saucepan, cover with water and boil for about 4 minutes. Whilst the barley is boiling, mix 50g of the best raw, organic sugar with the grated yellow peel of 2 lemons and leave for a few minutes for the lemon to flavour the sugar. When the boiling barley is ready, strain off the water and put it into a big jug, tip the sugar/lemon on top and mix together. Add 1 litre of boiling water and leave to completely cool. When cooled, put through a strainer and add the juice of the 2 lemons. Cool again in the fridge. It tastes divine.

My kids always gravitate towards cordials and juices that are loaded with sugar or artificial sweeteners. Try them on this – another great old-fashioned drink that is really easy to make, although it takes a little longer. This one is so eco-friendly it doesn't even leave much for the compost!

No-waste Apple Juice:

Peel and core 2kg of organic apples (sweet are best unless you have a very sour palette). Put the peelings and cores into a bowl and save the rest of the apples (you can make a fresh fruit salad or just eat the chunks). Add a small piece of cinnamon, 2 cloves and a half-inch of chopped fresh ginger. Grate the yellow rind of 1 organic lemon and mix with 80g of the best raw, organic sugar so the lemon flavours the sugar. Add to the apple mix and stir. Pour 2 litres of boiling water over the apple mix and leave for at least 8 hours. Strain, cool in fridge and drink. Yummy!

Sprouts

No, not the soggy green things you over boil for Christmas dinner but sprouted seeds – one of the most amazing wonder foods. You probably remember when you were a child covering a little jam jar of water with muslin and growing your own little seeds, or making mustard and cress on a bit of soggy felt. Well, it's all the same principle and it's so worth doing.

Sprouted seeds are one of the most concentrated sources of vitamins, minerals, amino acids, proteins and enzymes. They cost next to nothing, they're organic and you can add them to salads and sandwiches all year round. Make sure you buy organic seeds to sprout, of course. The easiest to start with are alfalfa, aduki beans and mung beans, but you can also sprout broccoli seeds, brown and green lentils, red clover seeds, rocket seeds and unhulled sunflower seeds.

You don't even need any special equipment to start sprouting but you can get a professional glass kit comprising two or three 0.75 litre glass jars with stainless steel mesh tops, drainage rack and glazed ceramic drip tray. Then you just rinse the seeds twice a day and invert the jars. Find out more about the above and lots more sprouting kits and organic seeds, from www. wholisticresearch.com.

Tips for feminine care:

A menstrual cup. I have found it invaluable in reducing the amount I lose during my 'moon' and it reduces pain. Washable sanitary towels/ pantyliners also reduce waste in the environment and are more comfortable for me.

If I had a magic wand, I would …

Listen to my instinct right from the word go!

HATTY – MUM OF FIVE AND FOUNDER OF SALTSHACK (HIMALAYAN SALT)

The great wheat debate

It's likely that you or someone you know is allergic or intolerant to wheat. Alarming, isn't it? It's hard to believe that such a staple food, and one that has dominated our diet for so many years, can be bad for us. I have a girlfriend whose stomach blows up as if she were five months pregnant if she takes one bite of a bread roll, and another friend who, after many years of headaches, bloating, irritable bowel syndrome (IBS), wind and acne, has finally cut out wheat and is glowing with health and vitality.

Wheat contains gluten and often it's that protein that is the baddie, as it can be very difficult to digest. Many people have some level of intolerance to gluten but some cope better than others. Often people feel better when they exclude it from their diet, even for a short time. However, gluten intolerance is not to be confused with the very serious gluten allergy: coeliac disease. Sufferers from that condition really must avoid gluten completely and forever.

I don't believe the solution is as simple as suggesting that everyone give up all bread products forever. I think that one of the problems is the way bread is now produced. Go and look at the ingredients of the average so-called 'healthy' loaf, whether brown or white, on the supermarket shelf. Even one that claims to be free from artificial preservatives and colourings is likely to contain a heap of stuff apart from wheat flour, yeast and gluten, including hydrogenated vegetable oil, salt, emulsifier, spirit vinegar, mono- and DA glycerides of fatty acids, and treacle or sugar/sweetener. No wonder a loaf lasts for up to a week. I find the best way is to get a bread maker and make your own wholegrain, or even mixed-grain, bread.

The great advantage of having your own bread maker is that you can experiment with different types of wholegrain. Spelt is an ancient grain that is more easily digestible by many people who are intolerant of wheat.

You can also make your own wheat and gluten-free bread but you'll need to be a bit more creative with the recipes. Sweeten it with honey instead of sugar and chuck in lots of hemp/poppy/sesame/pumpkin/sunflower seeds to increase your essential fatty acid intake and make it taste of something; otherwise it can be quite bland. I always use honey or agave syrup to sweeten any bread I make instead of sugar and use organic unsalted butter instead of margarine. I usually reduce the amount of salt quoted in the recipe as well. Also, go to the healthfood shop or organic supplier to buy your grains and try to get organic yeast. Bear in mind, too, that homemade bread has none of the preservatives of the shop-bought stuff, so you'll need to keep it in an airtight container and eat it within two days.

For those times when you've run out of yeast or other ingredients, the good news is that there are some great alternatives available in the shops. Look for the Terence Stamp range (yes, the actor with the gorgeous blue eyes) of wheat and gluten-free foods. Try to find a local bread shop that will make one hundred per cent rye bread, since many of the supermarket brands are only part rye, part wheat and gluten. Try pumper-nickel bread, hemp, buckwheat and, if you can find it, a ready-made spelt loaf.

Most supermarkets now also have a gluten-free sec-tion, offering chocolate bars, biscuits and cakes. These are wheat and gluten-free but that doesn't necessar-ily mean they're particularly healthy. They are often highly processed and contain high levels of salt, sugar (or sugar substitutes) and flavourings.

Cereals

When it comes to cereals there are some good ranges of organic muesli but it's very easy to make your own with organic oats, fruit, nuts and seeds.

Muesli:

2 cups oats

1 cup oats, dry-toasted

1 cup each of chopped almonds, desiccated coconut, chopped apricots, raisins

Gluten-free muesli:

Mix together 1 cup each of:

millet flakes   brown rice flakes

dry toasted buckwheat flakes

chopped hazelnuts   sunflower seeds

chopped apricots and raisins

Oats are good, so porridge for breakfast is fantastic (add fruit, nuts, seeds and yoghurt if you like) and cook with rice milk so you have a dairy-free porridge that doesn't need sweetening. Oats are still best avoided if you have gluten sensitivity, so remember that when you're knocking up flapjacks sweetened with honey and raisins.

Rice cakes, rye crackers and corn cakes (organic and unsalted if possible) are good for snacks with hummus. Use brown rice instead of white and, for some really interesting alternatives to rice and even couscous (which we tend to forget is a wheat product), try quinoa. It's something of a well-kept secret. It cooks in no time and can be eaten instead of rice and pasta, or can be added to casseroles and risottos. You can do the same with millet and buckwheat.

Sweet stuff

Trust me, I'm no domestic goddess. But when my kids (and I) crave something sweet, and I'm trying not to be too imperfect, one of my favourite things to knock up is what I call 'Sweetie Balls'. I must give the credit here to Carol Vorderman. In *Detox for Life* (Virgin Books), she calls them Marzipan Balls.

Sweetie Balls recipe:

Finely grind two cupfuls of almonds, knead with honey and a tiny amount of water till it forms a smooth paste.

Form small balls and roll them in ground cinnamon.

These are so easy to make and everyone loves them (as long as you don't have a nut allergy, obviously). I've even made a batch of balls, divided them into sixes or eights, wrapped them in that iridescent cellophane stuff tied with a ribbon – as my healthy contribution to the church fête cake stall. It's the closest we come to handmade chocolates.

Because I'm imperfect I must confess that my kids do eat actual sweets too. I just can't be perfect enough to keep them away from the little treasures but I make sure that, ninety-eight per cent of the time, the sweets are organic and free from the really hair-raising colourings and chemical additives. Healthfood shops do a good range of treats. Candy Tree produce excellent corn syrup candies. They are proper round lollies on a stick so the kids think they're getting the real deal. Just Wholefoods make VegeBears, organic, gelatine-free fruit jellies and fruit gums.

Talking chocolate

It is of course technically a superfood. It's so emotive and powerful and, of course, I'm not going to suggest we all eat loads of chocolate, but I'm not going to say give it up, either. It's well documented that it lifts our spirits and improves our sense of well-being. The key is: don't guzzle the whole box. I also think there's a huge difference between eating your average sugar, fat and chemical laden 'choco' bar from the local news-agent and eating a square or two of really high quality chocolate.

The Europeans are good at this. French chocolate is, by and large, far superior to ours and, even if you buy a household name brand over there, you'll find it tastes less sickly sweet. They just won't stand for it. Have organic chocolate if possible and the higher the cocoa solid ratio, the better it is. Opt for organic, seventy per cent cocoa, dark chocolate and you need only a couple of squares to feel you've had a treat. www.greenandblacks.com; www.divinechocolate.com. Raw chocolate is wonderful for vegans. Try www.detoxyourworld.com.

Dieting makes you fat

As a rule, I don't believe diets work. You would be pressed flat if you lay under the stack of books in my house about losing weight. My weight has been up and down like a yo-yo for many years and I've tried most diets. They can be a quick fix or a fast track, but it's what happens when you resume normality that matters. What's your lifestyle? How healthily do you eat? Do you eat what are, for you, the right foods? Do you exercise? Usually, unless your mindset has changed, you'll go back to all your old habits and the weight will pile back on.

I've already referred to the fantastic Carol Vorderman's *Detox for Life* and there are many books on the subject. She is often quoted as saying that she tried many diets and nothing worked until she came across the detox concept when she realised that food is linked with emotions and that we can't just starve ourselves. Afterwards, she changed her way of eating for good. For me the 'light bulb' moment came when I went on a 'juice retreat' and lost half a stone in a really healthy way in seven days. www.juicemaster.com.

Everyone needs to be in tune with their body and aware of its unique needs. What you put in as fuel and for enjoyment purposes should feel right to you. Only you know when you're overloading or feeling bloated or lacking energy. It's a great idea to detoxify your system, cleanse it and then start again. When you do a controlled fast for a few days you give your body a chance to recuperate and, when you start eating again, it's incredible how you actually notice what you're putting in your mouth. There's no way you would break a fast by eating a fry-up, so it gives you the opportunity to really taste your food and notice its effects.

This is just a bit of fun, one of those emails that do the rounds:

The Stress Diet

This is a specially formulated diet from the USA designed to help women cope with the stress that builds during the day:

Breakfast: 1 grapefruit, 1 slice whole-wheat toast, 1 cup of skimmed milk

Lunch: 1 small portion lean, steamed chicken, 1 cup spinach, 1 cup herbal tea, 1 Hershey's Kiss

Afternoon Snack: Rest of the Hershey's Kisses in the bag, 1 tub Häagen-Dazs ice cream with chocolate chip topping

Dinner: 4 glasses of wine (red or white), 2 loaves garlic bread, 1 family sized supreme pizza, 3 Snickers bars

Late night snack: 1 whole Sara Lee Cheesecake (eaten directly from the freezer)

Remember — Stressed spelt backwards is Desserts.

Send this to four women and you will lose 2 pounds. Send this to all the women you know (or ever knew) and you will lose 10 pounds. If you delete this message, you will gain 10 pounds immediately.

That's why I had to pass this on. I didn't want to risk it, so my weight loss will depend on how many people read the book! Remember, it is called *Im*perfectly Natural Woman!

If I had a magic wand, I would …

… meditate twice a day and make love more often.

INGRID –

HOME EDUCATING MUM OF TWO

Essential fatty acids and dietary supplements

In a lovely ideal world, we wouldn't need supplements to our diets at all, be they vitamins, minerals or essential fatty acids (EFAs), but we all know the reality: diets today are, shall we say, less than perfect. I see supplements as a kind of damage limitation.

It can be totally overwhelming to walk into a health-food store and see the huge range of vitamins and minerals available. We'd be rattling if we took one of every variety. It is very difficult to know exactly what our bodies need. If the store has a nutritionist, you can be tested to determine which minerals are lacking, or you can send off blood and hair samples to give a clearer picture of what's needed; but, as a general rule, (and this is a sweeping statement) I'd say listen to your body and your own intuition. If you're feeling under stress or reckon you're about to get ill, up the ante a bit and take some protective measures.

As a rule of thumb I'd suggest you consider taking a good multivitamin tablet every day, some vitamin C (more when you're fighting an infection) and the one I recommend for all of us, particularly women, essential fatty acids.

EFAs are naturally occurring, unsaturated fats, some of which are not produced by the human body. There are two very important ones, Omega 6 and Omega 3, and without these many bodily functions would not be possible. Our bodies use linolenic acid to make another two EFAs, docosahexaenoic acid (DHA) and eicosapentaenoic acid (EPA). These are found in fish oil as well.

One of the major roles of EFAs in the body is as structural components of cell membranes. EFAs are also vital for the formation of hormone-like substances called prostaglandins, which are crucial for a variety of functions including steroid hormone production. 'Essential' is the operative word here. That's the technical bit. In short, your body loves EFAs, found in fish oils and in low levels in animal products such as liver and kidney – but how much herring, mackerel, sardines and fresh tuna can you eat? And how full of toxins are those foods, anyway? Apart from that, when was the last time your other half or five-year-old asked for liver? It's a difficult one.

There have been so many reports recently that suggest we need these EFAs to help with brain function (even to help with depression and Alzheimer's disease). Recent research suggests that DHA in the diet of our ancestors was an important factor in the evolution of human intelligence. Children who are given supplements on a regular basis consistently perform better in IQ tests, and it also has a positive effect on children with learning difficulties and behavioural problems. It is confusing, though, working out your DHAs from your EFAs but the excellent website www.dha-in-mind.com explains it well.

Intake of DHA and EPA has declined in the UK and other countries with a Western diet over the past fifty years. This is shown by levels of DHA in breast milk, which are much lower than they used to be. We are eating less fish and offal. Modern farming practices have led to a reduction in the DHA levels of eggs and meat and we now eat more food that is high in another Omega family, the Omega 6s. Experts now advise us to redress the balance and eat more Omega 3s, including DHA.

So, we know we need it, but how do we get it? The obvious sources are oily fish and fish oils, though there are concerns about fish nowadays. The seas are so polluted and these types of fish seem to absorb pollutants such as mercury more readily than others. The problem with fish oil supplements (e.g. cod liver) is that it is not always the 'purest' or the most complete mix of the oils. We're a bit more sophisticated now when it comes to how our fish oils are processed and I'd recommend getting a supplement that's been through a purification process. Check with your friendly health-store person rather than pick the standard supermarket cod liver supplements. The best I've found are called MorEPA, which come in capsules and even mini-capsules (www.minami-nutrition.com). You can buy them from www.healthyandessential.com.

But what if you're vegetarian? A good source is hemp oil and flaxseed oil. They both taste great on salads and have a really earthy flavour. Don't use in cooking though as the heat process destroys their goodness.

You can also buy 'good oils' for veggies such as The Groovy Food Company's Cool Oil (www.groovyfood.co.uk). It's a blend of organic seed oils – flax, hemp, pumpkin and evening primrose – that provide Omega 3, 6 and 9 in a 2:1:1 ratio. (Keep it in the fridge.) Udo's Choice is the market leader but has a heavier flavour and it's also available in a tablet form from www.udoschoice.co.uk.

If I had a magic wand, I would …

… find more time to relax, meditate, exercise and have fun.

I'd also like to recommend …

We create our lives by what we say and do. Allow everyone to express their anger, sadness and fears without 'dumping' on anyone else.

FELICITY – MUM OF ONE AND
FOUNDER OF NATUREKIDS

Nuts and seeds

I haven't yet mentioned the wonder that is a bowl of nuts and seeds. I don't mean salted peanuts but pretty much anything else will do.

Mixed seeds are really a wonder. Try to eat a bowl every day if you can. It's so simple. Get a little coffee grinder (use a separate one unless you want coffee-flavoured seeds) and grind up a handful of sunflower, hemp, pumpkin and sesame, add a few linseeds and sprinkle the mix over cereals and yoghurt. Hemp seeds are fantastic. www.yorkshirehemp.com

For savoury snacks, you can't do better than a bowl of toasted seeds. They taste great and give you a real boost of the essential Omega 3 oils.

Toasted seed special:

Heat up a frying pan with a dash of olive oil and when it's hot, throw in any mix of seeds then drizzle a bit of tamari over them. Lightly toast until browned, cool and eat by the handful or as an addition to salads and sandwiches.

If I had a magic wand, I would …

Eat according to my 'Metabolic Type' even though it means cutting out a lot of the food I feel I don't have a problem with, and making sure I do my Chi stick exercises and some stretching every day.

DANI – FITNESS TRAINER

Manuka honey

Manuka honey really is a wonder food. It is antiseptic, healing and brilliant for sores and wounds.

Well, I knew of honey as a contraceptive aid (remember the craze of the honey cap in the eighties?), so it didn't surprise me that it was useful for more than just eating.

Manuka honey smoothie hangover cure recipe:

Blend

2 teaspoons of manuka honey

half a banana

half a cup of chopped papaya

1 cup semi-skimmed milk or rice milk

3 teaspoons of natural yoghurt

Serve over ice cubes to cure your imperfectly natural hangover!

Manuka honey comes from bees that collect pollen from the manuka bush (*Leptospermum Scoparium*), which grows wild in the lovely land of New Zealand. That part of the southern hemisphere is one of the least polluted areas on earth, so we're talking happy bees here. The Maoris have used the honey for generations, both externally and internally, and modern medicine is now reconsidering its uses in the light of new research into the properties of this amazing stuff. I've read about its use in hospitals, where it has been applied directly to wounds, a process known as apitherapy (from *Apis*, which is the honeybee genus).

In the shops, you'll see it marked 'UMF', which means 'Unique Manuka Factor', and it's a kind of industry-standard grading. The honey is tested for its antibacterial properties and awarded a grading, usually between 5 and 15. It's then deemed 'active'. The best stuff, used in apitherapy, will have a grading above 10. Get the highest UMF rating you can afford and always get 'active' for extra antibacterial properties.

I've applied manuka honey directly to burns and, when one of my boys had a splinter in his foot that became infected we left the bottle of toxic prescription antibiotics on the shelf and just waited for a few days while we tried applying active 10+ manuka honey. It cleared up within two days. I also have a friend who wishes to remain nameless who applied it to his painless haemorrhoids – cured! A bit sticky, but much better than over-the-counter 'pile cream'.

Active manuka honey is fantastic to eat and, for information on its therapeutic properties, check out www.naturesnectar.com and www.manukahoney.co.uk.

If I had a magic wand, I would …

… never desire a glass of wine again.

TIGGY – COMMERCIALS PRODUCER

Water filters

Since we were all warned many years back that tap water is bad for us, we've spent millions of pounds on expensive bottled mineral water that costs more than petrol and can cost a fortune in treatments because our backs and shoulders have been put out by lugging six litres of it home from the supermarket!

Bottled water companies have indeed triumphed. British sales alone are worth around £2 billion a year – but are we buying it because it tastes better, is convenient to carry around, or because it's better for our health?

There is no doubt that water is essential and we need lots of it. The current advice to consume a recommended eight glasses a day is, to my mind, the minimum. Of course there's the hazard of needing to pee all the time but it's interesting that, once you start drinking lots of water, your body seems to adjust after a day or so and you don't need to go to the loo quite so often. I have several friends who swear by drinking loads of water as their main aid to losing weight.

Always drink water at room temperature, though: icy cold water is a shock to the system. It chills the stomach, making the process of absorbing nutrients less effective.

So what kind of water should we be drinking? We all know it's pointless buying a bottle of 'table' water. It isn't natural and contains no minerals. Remember the episode of *Only Fools and Horses* where Del Boy discovers an ancient well in the garden? They decide to bottle the water from it and call it 'Peckham Springs'. Of course it turned out to be no more than a burst water pipe, so Del was rebottling the water from the local water authority that was already coming out of his kitchen tap!

> *In time and with water, everything changes.*
>
> LEONARDO DA VINCI

So what are the minerals in bottled mineral water? Usually, calcium, magnesium, sodium and sodium bicarbonate, but the levels will vary depending on where they spring from – literally. The mineral water companies and the National Mineral Water

Association would have us believe that their water tastes better and has great health benefits. The World Health Organisation, many GPs and of course your local water authority, would disagree and suggest that mineral water is no better for you than tap water unless you have a low dietary intake of certain minerals. In which case you could benefit from drinking water with high levels of a particular mineral but that of course might not taste as good. It also starts to prompt the question, 'Hold on, then. If I need certain minerals, can't I supplement my diet in other ways?'

The problem is that, once opened, bottled mineral water loses its freshness very quickly and becomes a breeding ground for bacteria. I was buying a large plastic bottle of mineral water, having a couple of swigs and then leaving it in the car. There it would sit in the hot sunshine for a couple days, breeding bugs and generally 'going off'. Also I began to wonder, even before it got cooked on my dashboard, how long this stuff had been lurking on shop shelves.

Filtered water is of course the option many people use instead of buying the bottled stuff. The problem with our tap water, we all know, is not what it contains 'naturally' but what's been added. Well, in some areas it's fluoride, which, needless to say, I'm hugely against, but in every case there will be chlorine and chemicals to aid purification, plus, some critics say, traces of pesticides, heavy metals (such as calcium and lead), nitrates and even asbestos, as well as fair amounts of bacteria.

Someone suggested I try an under-sink reverse osmosis water filter and this has revolutionised my water drinking habits. First, gone are the heavy bottles of water; second, gone is the hassle of remembering to bring in unopened bottles from the car; and third, now there are fewer plastic bottles clogging up the environment. By the way, the plastic always was a bit of an issue with me, not just from an environmental point of view. Some schools of thought maintain that substances in the plastic leach into the water over time, creating another potential pollutant. There are some ardent bottled water drinkers who advocate drinking only water stored in glass.

The reverse osmosis water filter from Dryden Aqua (www.drydenaqua.co.uk) is the one I found to be most cost-effective. The filtration bit is meant to last for a couple of years, depending on how much you use, and it comes with a little monitor so that you can check the water yourself. Replacements are around £50 – well worth it compared with what I'd been spending on the bottled variety every year. It has also made a huge difference to my kettle. I used to need to clean it out every few weeks with vinegar and replace it every two years but since I had the reverse osmosis filter fitted, I've seen no staining or scaling and the water boils quickly and tastes better.

It's also worth contacting your local water company to find out the mineral content and fluoridation content of your water supply.

If you still want to buy bottled water try to keep it in the fridge, not the car, and buy glass bottles wherever possible. My favourites are the French ones, Evian, Volvic and Perrier. San Pellegrino, the Italian one, is also nice. You can also drink Deeside Water, the mineral water that is said to give the Royal Family their

longevity as it flows near Balmoral. www.deesidewater
.co.uk.

Natural cures for common ailments

This book is not meant to be a medical directory or even an alternative 'cure-all'. I'm no doctor or expert but I can tell you what I find helpful when I'm feeling under the weather.

Health professionals would have you believe that all over-the-counter medicines are totally safe but, as recently as 2004, a friend of mine in the States came across a list of drugs that were being recalled urgently. Each contained phenylpropanolamine, which had been linked to increased haemorrhagic stroke (bleeding in the brain). The recalled products included common, household name, store cupboard 'staples' such as cough and cold medicines, expectorants and powders, preparations for sinus and nasal congestion, even some children's chewable tablets. The next time you want to take some of these over-the-counter drugs, or pop a headache pill, just check out (a) the list of ingredients and (b) the possible side effects (that is, if you've got a spare half hour to read it). Fortunately, there are alternatives.

Colds, sore throats, coughs

When I feel a cold coming on I take vitamin C, usually the crystals – sodium ascorbate – at least 1,000mg, twice a day. I really believe vitamin C taken at the onset of any infection helps and, if you do overdo it and take too much for your body to process, you may just have mild diarrhoea, though it hasn't happened to me so far. Biocare make a tiny bottle of micellised vitamin C. Basically, Vitasorb C is a high-strength liquid, which is an excellent way of getting it into your system without the addition of too many gelling and other agents (see www.biocare.co.uk).

I usually take one garlic capsule and a zinc tablet too for a few days and drink copious amounts of honey, lemon and ginger. I make up a big pan of one or two chopped lemons, a big chunk of fresh ginger and hot water. I boil it, then simmer for ten minutes or so and sip with one teaspoon of, preferably, manuka honey, added once it's cool. Ginger, by the way, is a wonderful spice to have in stock. In Southeast Asia and India it is still considered to be an essential ingredient of the daily diet as a protection against disease and an aid to digestion. Drink freshly extracted fruit and veg juices, too.

Epsom salts or Dead Sea salts are great for adding to bathwater, particularly if you feel you're coming down with a cold. Have a warm bath, put in a large cupful of salts and a couple of drops of essential oil, wrap up warm and go to bed. You should wake up feeling quite different.

Tea tree oil is never far from my side when I've got a virus or an infection lurking. I put a few drops on a tissue and breathe in the aroma and leave a few drops on my pillow at night or in a bowl on the radiator or oil burner. For a sore throat or when I feel I'm losing my voice, I put one drop in a glass of water, shake it around and then gargle. It's brilliantly antiseptic.

Coughs can be a devil to treat and I don't believe any of the commercial brands available in the chemists actually work, even if you're prepared to put up with the chemicals and their side effects. There are some natural alternatives, though. Try Ainsworths, www.ainsworths.com or Helios, www.helios.co.uk.

Homemade cough syrup recipes:

Steep 1oz of thyme leaf in 1 cup of boiling water, cover it and leave it to cool.

Strain and mix with ¾ tablespoon of honey. Take a teaspoon whenever you need it and it will keep in a glass jar in the fridge for a few days. Children usually love it.

Sugar and onion syrup:

Both onion and honey are anti-inflammatory and anti-microbial. Try coating a small onion in brown sugar or honey and leaving it overnight on a saucer. In the morning strain off the juice and soothe your cough!

For bronchitis:

1 clove garlic finely chopped in manuka honey twice a day, taken off the spoon and swallowed quickly or on bread.

For high temperatures:

Try lime flower tea with manuka.

Coughs and sore throats:

Prepare a warm drink of carrageen seaweed and chamomile tea. Simmer carrageen in a big pan (1tbs to 1pt water) for 20 minutes. Take off heat, add chamomile. Strain after 10 minutes. Add honey and keep warm in flask. It's extraordinarily soothing on the throat.

Bump up the vitamin C and echinacea.

Organic essential oils – ¾ drops in a burner, or 1 drop on clothing near face, or under blanket (see above). Oils to use:

- lavender and chamomile if you feel agitated and tender at night, maybe also with headache, stuffed nose, little cough
- pine for bad respiratory problems.
- eucalyptus if it's even worse
- sage for the throat
- thyme for the chest

More suggestions for colds, coughs and breathing problems:

- eucalyptus and lavender oils to help breathing and aid relaxation
- raise head
- stay hydrated
- cut out any dairy or wheat in the diet
- get a vapouriser
- unless you're a veggie – chicken soup
- boil about a pint of water with juice of at least 4 lemons, chucking in a bit of zest and the lemon halves, too, some cloves, some ginger and at least 4 cloves of crushed garlic. let it simmer a bit, then strain off the 'juice', add some honey and drink it hot.

Also, for any kind of breathing problems, keep some peppermint oil on hand. Put a couple of drops on the back of your hand and 'kiss' it (don't lick it – yuk). You can feel your airways opening up in moments.

Steam:

Steam works a treat on any respiratory problems. For young children, fill the bath and get the whole room steamed up but, for yourself, boil a kettle of water, add a few drops of tea tree oil or, better still, crush a couple of eucalyptus leaves. Position your face about ten inches from the hot water (being careful not to scald yourself) and drape a towel over your head to keep in the steam. It not only works as a brilliant decongestant but you'll get a great facial in the process. My kids usually shout, 'Oh, look, Mummy's boiling her head again!'

Drape a blanket over chairs and sit underneath, breathing in steam from a bowl of boiling water standing in a large bowl, three times a day.

Steaming is good for headaches, too, and Tiger Balm applied sparingly on the temples will help (get the natural ones rather than petrochemical based). Also, drink lots of water – it's amazing the number of people with chronic headaches who are cured when they start drinking two litres a day.

Hay fever

If you are a sufferer, try a couple of things before you hit the antihistamines. First, there is the local honey theory. This works on the premise that we're often intolerant to certain pollens, which may be grown locally. Get hold of some locally grown honey and eat it as you normally would, preferably in February/ March before the hay fever season starts. Hopefully, if it's grown within a few miles of your home, it will correspond to the pollens you're allergic to and you'll be desensitised when the season kicks off.

Once you've got the symptoms, try coating the inside of the nostrils with olive oil or apricot kernel oil, which will protect the sensitive mucus membranes from the flying particles. Try HayMax from health stores as a non-petroleum alternative to Vaseline. www.haybalm. f2s.com.

Cystitis and thrush

This is one I know about, as it often flares up in pregnancy and is utterly horrible if you get a bad attack. Don't even think about prescription drugs: they can increase the pain and discomfort and even be the cause of it. Cranberries are the best natural remedy for cystitis, and women often think it's OK to buy a bag of sweetened ones and munch their way through them in the name of health. You should try to get unsweetened cranberry juice and drink 16fl.oz a day in addition to at least two litres of water. The more water you drink to dilute the urine, the less painful it will be. Cranberry supplements in capsule form taken with meals are good too.

Lemon barley water will neutralise the acid but again, avoid the sweetened version and make your own if you can.

Avoid dairy, wheat and sugar for a day or two if possible and boost your intake of vitamin C. Eat lots of apricots, green peppers, broccoli and citrus fruit.

Obviously, avoid any chemical irritants such as soap and bubble bath, and use a few drops of essential oil in the bath. Bergamot is meant to be good for thrush and vaginal itching. Sandalwood oil is also very useful for the urinary system and lavender and chamomile oils may help. Tea tree oil can also be inserted into the vaginal area, but be careful to use only one drop in about a teaspoon of virgin olive oil (otherwise it will sting like hell!).

Take probiotic supplements as long as you're not having antibiotics (if you are, take probiotics afterwards), and you can use a regular probiotic capsule as a pessary – it's far less messy than over-the-counter pessaries! (I've also heard of inserting a clove of garlic but must confess I haven't tried that one in case it doesn't make its way out again!) Ideally, we'd be able to eat enough live yoghurt not to need probiotics but that's unrealistic, so take a good supplement of acidophilus in powder or capsule form but remember that most need to be kept in the fridge.

Digestive upsets

Let's face it, we all have times when we get food poisoning, a really nasty stomach bug or a self-inflicted dodgy bottom, usually from the excesses of rich food and drink. The best way to deal with them is just to let nature take its course. I would definitely avoid any medication that suppresses the problem. After all, your body is trying to rid itself of toxins and poisons, so let it do its work.

It's interesting to observe animals when they're ill. They usually retire quietly and consume nothing at all. A self-imposed fast will work wonders and allow your digestive system to rest. When you begin to feel better and hungry again, drink plenty of filtered water and allow yourself the blandest of foods, plain cooked rice, ripe pears and loads of water. Introduce other foods slowly to allow the detoxification of your system to continue.

If it's just a mild digestive upset you won't go wrong with peppermint tea or, if you can get it, peppermint essence. As I've already mentioned, ginger is also good for digestive problems. You can chew on a piece of fresh ginger, make a ginger tea, even have a ginger biscuit as long as the problem won't be compounded by an intake of wheat and sugar.

Minor burns

For minor burns neat lavender oil is amazing. It's not instant but, trust me, it works – just a drop or two directly on the burn. Aloe vera 'juice' is also amazing.

You just slice open the leaf and put the sap directly on any skin irritations or burns.

Sleep

If you are an insomniac, no amount of suggesting you relax and have a milky drink will have any effect. However, if the problem is just that you occasionally feel your mind is too active, I have a couple of suggestions that are so simple you'll either be using them already, or wonder why I'm bothering to write them down because they're so daft. First, if you have a TV or computer in your bedroom, remove it. It's not only the electromagnetic frequencies that are the problem but I believe the bedroom should be for sleep and sex, and sleep and sex alone! If you fill your mind with a horror movie or even the news late at night, it's obvious that it will be harder to relax into counting sheep.

The best little exercise I learned was to clear my mind of all the worries and thoughts of the day. Writing it all down is good, 'journalling' as the self-help books call it, but I am often too lazy to find a pen. So I visualise a big sack and I 'see' myself putting all my worries in there at night: the intricate schedule for the next day, the fears, the lot. Each time another thought or fear pops up I slip it into the bag. Then I imagine hanging the sack at the foot of the bed so that the sensible and rational part of my subconscious brain knows I'm not trying to kid myself that it's simple to erase all worries and that they will be there ready and waiting after a night's rest.

> *Man is ill because he is never still.*
>
> PARACELSUS

Sometimes I use a relaxation tape – slightly imperfect, I know, as it goes against my rules of minimal electrical equipment. Make sure you like the voice of the person reading the meditation, or it will really grate on you. You may find a type of music that is sleep-inducing for you. If you want to try sleep-inducing foods, then obviously avoid cheese, coffee and wine, and go for bananas and lettuce! Chamomile tea is relaxing, if not exactly soporific and, if you can bear it, green tea works. We all know of its antioxidant properties but it also contains a natural relaxant, L-theanine. The herbal remedies valerian and passiflora can also help.

Also, I know it sounds obvious but we should sleep in darkness. Our bodies are designed to sleep when it's dark and wake far earlier than most of us actually do, when it's light. Unless we live in very remote areas, we don't experience true darkness because there are always street lights or intermittent lights from neighbouring houses or passing cars. Even with eyes closed, light will interfere with the brain's natural sleep patterns. We probably aren't going to change our lifestyles but at least we can turn off that bedside lamp and draw the curtains. Also try the wonderful 'Stars', a blend for sweet dreams from www.speciallittlepeople.co.uk.

A new supplement called Asphalia has been developed by the internationally recognised Coghill Research Laboratories. It's a plant extract that produces natural melatonin and users report significantly improved sleep patterns. www.asphalia.co.uk.

Anxiety, depression and SAD

One kind word can warm three winter months.

JAPANESE PROVERB

Of course, serious mental health problems can't be classed as a common ailment and must be treated professionally but so many people suffer from mild depression and anxiety, which can include anything from PMS, or a miserable case of the winter blues, to a minor case of post-natal depression. There are a few well-documented, mood-boosting natural remedies but it's worth checking with a practitioner and, if you are taking prescribed medication, always check before supplementing it with complementary remedies of any kind.

If you're suffering from seasonal affective disorder (SAD), consider renting or buying a light therapy box.

We need our daylight as a fish needs water and, if it's a dull winter's day or we're working long hours under horrible fluorescent lighting, a dose of full spectrum light works wonders. You can find out more about their therapeutic effects at www.apollo-health.co.uk or www.wholisticresearch.com. Both companies sell a range of lamps and lightboxes including portable ones.

It goes without saying that exercise is a mood booster too. Even just a twenty minute brisk walk in the fresh air can change your perspective on everything.

Look at your intake of essential fatty acids (see the section 'Essential fatty acids and dietary supplements' in 'Let food be your medicine' above). Fish oils are very effective at easing and treating depression, especially when it has a hormonal origin. Nutritionally, supplements of vitamin B6 should be helpful, preferably as part of the B complex.

Buy foods that are rich in B vitamins and eat them in as unprocessed a form as you can. Get yourself a good multivitamin/mineral supplement too but bear in mind that the benefits of vitamin therapy may take time to kick in. Consider also Vitex agnus-castus and raspberry leaf tea, which will help to balance hormones. Aromatherapy may help too, as essential oils can be very mood-enhancing. Get a friend to recommend a really good aromatherapist and make sure they know how you're feeling so that they can mix the perfect balance of oils.

Bach flower remedies may also help. The correct remedy is hard to suggest off the cuff, but looking at www.bachcentre.com and browsing the different remedies to see what sounds closest to your present state of mind may help.

Homoeopathy

You should also consider seeing a homoeopath. Homoeopathic treatment offers a healing system that will deal with pretty much every complaint.

It's worth getting a recommendation to a good local homoeopath or consider going to one of the college clinics where you'll get a reduced rate. It's definitely worth keeping a well stocked homoeopathic remedy kit too. At least make sure you have Arnica for bruising and shock, Apis for bites and stings, and Nux Vomica for digestive upsets. See www.ainsworths. com; 020 7935 5330.

Another excellent supplier, which also offers a boxed kit, is Helios Pharmacy (www.helios.co.uk; 01892 537254). To find a registered homoeopath in your area, try the Society of Homeopaths (www.homeopathy-soh.org) or the Alliance of Registered Homoeopaths (www.a-r-h.org).

> *The art of healing comes from nature and not from the physician. Therefore, the physician must start from nature with an open mind.*
>
> PARACELSUS

Herbs

At one time, we'd have needed to go foraging in fields and hedgerows to make up our own herbs and herbal remedies. Now there are companies that sell dried herbs, tinctures, herbal teas and pills. Most good health food shops stock a range of Bioforce products and they produce an excellent Quick Herbal Guide. (See www.bioforce.co.uk.)

Here are some that I keep in my herbal medicine cabinet:

- hypericum – antiviral action, especially appropriate for the nervous system;

- echinacea – take internally as tincture and externally as cream; antiviral and a boost to the immune system;

- gingko biloba, for poor circulation – improves blood supply to extremities;

- ginger – warming blood tonic that boosts circulation;

- vinca minor – increases tone of blood vessels;

- feverfew – for headaches, can protect against migraine headaches if taken daily

St John's wort is often recommended for depression, although it can have contraindications with other medication (notably in the case of tissue rejection after a transplant), and it may not be suitable for breast-feeding mums, possibly due to its hypericin content.

It's helpful to keep a quick-reference guide alongside a couple of herbal remedies in your bathroom cabinet but be aware that certain herbs do have contraindications. It's best to check with your doctor if you're taking any prescribed medicines and, despite my anecdote about my pregnancy herbs, remember I was under supervision. On no account take herbs without advice if you are pregnant. Plants and herbs are powerful. They are the basis of all our modern medication. Treat them with respect and don't exceed the recommended dose.

There are also a few good mail order suppliers:

Hambleden Herbs. www.hambledenherbs.co.uk.

Halzephron Herb Farm who also produce a helpful free guide to which herbal medicines could help you, *The Natural Alternative* by Deborah Fowler, available from www.halzherb.com.

Neal's Yard Remedies are a good source. www.nealsyardremedies.com.

G Baldwin & Co for herbs, teas, tinctures and flower remedies. www.baldwins.co.uk; 020 7703 5550.

Guilty secrets and imperfections:

I do find comfort in food. My imperfections are too numerous to mention but include worrying too much about my figure, which drives my husband nuts. Self-acceptance is my goal.

TIGGY – COMMERCIALS PRODUCER

Touch therapies

The power of touch is amazing. I believe we can actually boost our immune systems when we are stroked and touched. It can help with our response to pain and increase our feelings of well-being.

Most of us don't think of treating ourselves to a therapeutic touch session. We just expect our bodies to do their thing day in day out and feel greatly miffed when we develop a pain or pull a muscle. In truth, if we all had regular treatments as a preventive measure, we would probably have far fewer aches and pains and we'd certainly have an increased sense of well-being.

All the many forms and styles of touch therapies have different things to offer for different people. Don't wait until you're racked with pain. There are too many to mention, so I've just listed my favourites. Ask for a voucher for birthday or Christmas and redeem it with a treatment.

Bowen Technique

'Bowen is not a miracle,' said the Bowen practitioner (trying to alleviate the intense sacroiliac pain I was suffering during my pregnancy) 'but it is amazing!' An Australian, Tom Bowen, working alongside osteopaths, devised it before developing the treatment on animals.

I'd been recommended to try Bowen with this therapist who had a track record in successfully treating lower-back pain, RSI (repetitive strain injury), migraine, hay fever, arthritis, MS and worse. 'Sometimes one treatment is all that's needed,' she told me. Chequebook in hand, I firmly decided that I was all hers.

I lay down fully clothed and she gently stimulated and 'rolled' muscles which, in turn (I'm told), stimulated a nervous response in my brain saying, 'Listen, brain, there's a problem here, please sort it.' With a Bowen treatment, it's actually your body that assesses the information and starts to take action. It's painless and I could hardly even feel it. After a few little 'moves', the therapist quietly left the room. This is the point where you may suspect there's a charlatan at work, but it's all for a good reason. Apparently, it allows the body's energies solo space in which to heal.

Twenty minutes later she had finished, leaving me alone again to 'cook', as she called it. I had to pace around the room and drink lots of water. Did Bowen persuade my body to heal its own muscular problems? Well, I had limped in to see her as if carrying the weight of the world on my lumber region, but after the session I leapt up the steps from the basement treatment room like the recipient of a veritable miracle from the New Testament!

I've since recommended many people to try the Bowen Technique, and to that practitioner. I have heard of many success stories from colleagues with tennis elbow, frozen shoulder, and even great news from a friend who has been cured of early onset arthritis and a neighbour who was told he'd never walk again but is now driving, walking and back on the golf course.

Our bodies are amazing and, as Hippocrates said, 'The body has the innate ability to heal itself, provided it's given the opportunity to do so.'

Bowen worked for me. It's honestly like a miracle, but do get a recommendation to a therapist if you can. A treatment usually costs around £45 but the beauty is that you rarely need many. For further information, look at www.thebowentechnique.com.

Aromatherapy

This was the first 'hands-on' treatment I ever had and it was bliss. I now have regular aromatherapy massages and use essential oils on a daily basis (see 'Save your skin').

It's probably the most popular treatment because it's usually affordable, there are loads of excellent therapists and its benefits are felt instantly. Try to find a holistic aromatherapist who uses the healing properties of essential oils and the wonderful aroma not only to relax and de-stress you but also to treat lots of different ailments, including physical and emotional problems.

For those of you who decide just to use essential oils at home, there is a wide range available. Always buy pure essential oils and then learn how to dilute them with a carrier oil. Never use them neat on the skin (with the exception of tea tree oil and lavender to dab on spots) and treat oils with care, since they are potent and can be dangerous in the wrong hands. Be aware that certain oils have contraindications for certain conditions. For example, many oils must be avoided in pregnancy including lavender and you may need to avoid some oils if you have high blood pressure. So, if you're at all unsure, try to see a practitioner first. In any case, read up on it.

For essential oils – www.essentiallyoils.com, www. eoco.org.uk, www.tisserand.com. To find a qualified aromatherapist, contact the Federation of Holistic Therapists, www.fht.org.uk. See also www.aromather-apycouncil.co.uk.

Craniosacral therapy

I hadn't come across this until I was in labour and my birth guru gave me craniosacral treatment throughout. It's basically very gentle manipulation, usually focusing on the skull. It aims to normalise the natural rhythms of the body to encourage the body's natural ability to self-heal. You barely feel a thing while you just lie back and allow the weight of your head to 'hang' in the hands of the therapist. The touch is very gentle and it's a lovely feeling. After a while you feel a sort of floating sensation.

Craniosacral therapy or cranial osteopathy are also brilliant for newborn babies, helping to heal birth trauma and to put back tiny little nerves and muscles that have shifted during the birth process. I know of one therapist who was consulted by a woman about her fourteen-month-old baby. This poor boy was red and screaming, sleeping very erratically and not eating well. Doctors could find no medical reason for his obvious discomfort. The cranial osteopath gently manipulated his skull and was convinced that he'd managed to shift a tiny trapped nerve that would have been pressing on the baby's brain. He had probably had a raging headache since his very difficult and lengthy birth but did not yet have the ability to communicate this fact. The relief was instant. The child relaxed, stopped crying and even managed a smile. At his check-up appointment one month later his mother reported that it was like having a different child. Even newborn babies respond really well to this treatment, which can also involve little movements on their tummy. Also it usually has a beneficial effect on colic and sleep problems.

For adults, it's excellent for neck and shoulder aches and pains, migraines and problems with circulation. The practitioner uses very gentle manipulation to help the blood flow and balance the lymphatic system.

As always, find a good practitioner. Try the Craniosacral Therapy Association (www.craniosacral. co.uk) or the Sutherland Society for a cranial osteopath (www.cranial.org.uk).

Reflexology

Yes, it's the fiddling-with-feet treatment. Apparently, the foot reflects the body of a seated person, with the toes relating to the head and the heel corresponding to the bottom. The instep area is like a map of the internal organs. For some reason, this absolutely brilliant diagnostic and therapeutic practice often gets a bad press. It may be because frequently it's offered at beauty salons and sometimes the masseurs are doing nothing more than that – massaging the feet. Actually, reflexology can hurt. The reflexologist stimulates certain points on the foot, using his or her thumbs and, as with the Bowen Technique, it is thought that this triggers the body to heal itself. When your energy (chi) is not flowing correctly and there is a blockage, you may feel a sharp stabbing pain. It's bearable (usually), so don't worry. If the practitioner really knows their stuff, they'll be able to diagnose conditions and potential problems from the points in the feet that correspond to different organs in the body.

Like acupuncture, reflexology has been used in China and India for thousands of years and the philosophy is that the life force, or what is known as prana in Indian practice, circulates in a rhythmic way around the body. If the energy is disrupted by injury, signals are transmitted down energy channels within the body to the feet. A trained therapist can then feel the affected areas by identifying points that feel like grains of sand under the skin. Hence, it can be an excellent diagnostic tool as well as actually dispersing the 'blockages' and cleansing the area. I suppose that when we were all running around over uneven ground without shoes, it was nature's way of keeping us healthy by doing its own type of reflexology.

In the hands of a fully qualified prenatal practitioner, reflexology is very safe in pregnancy. It's best to wait until twelve weeks, but, after that, regular treatments are one of the best indicators of your internal health. It can also be profoundly helpful in balancing the thyroid gland function, frequently out of kilter after childbirth, a contributor to postnatal depression.

For general use, it can alleviate anxiety, stress, skin disorders and some injuries.

Try to get a personal recommendation and check out the Association of Reflexologists, 01823 351010 (www.reflexology.org).

To conclude, I've gained benefits from all of these treatments, although for me, Bowen was the big revelation, even for serious muscular problems. So try them out if you can. If you just don't have the cash or you can't steal the time, get your partner or friend to give you a good rub down. It's all touch therapy!

natural home

> *When friends enter a home, they sense its personality and character, the family's style of living — these elements make a house come alive with a sense of identity, a sense of energy, enthusiasm and warmth, declaring, 'This is who we are, this is how we live.'*
>
> RALPH LAUREN

Get your house in order

Time to dust again
Time to caress my house,
To stroke all its surfaces
I want to think of it as a kind of lovemaking
… the chance to appreciate by touch
what I live with and cherish.

GUNILLA NORRIS

Cleaning and products

What our lovely, global chemical conglomerates don't
want us to know is that it's entirely possible to clean
things 'naturally'. That doesn't just mean eco-friendly
products, though they are fantastic for the most part,
but things that are dead cheap, natural and easily available. Once you change your philosophical approach,
it's so easy to do.

At home, we become so attuned to the whiffs and ambience of background chemicals in our everyday surroundings that we just don't notice them any more but, rest assured, they're still there, still seeping their way into your body and doing their work.

There is a school of thought that regards the gradual depletion of our immune systems over the past fifty years as an effect of the long-term infiltration of multiple man-made substances in our everyday environments. Just go old style and save cash and your health in the process. You'll need to stock up on:

- white vinegar (distilled if you can get it);
- bicarbonate of soda;
- soda crystals;
- borax (Boots chemists stock it);
- household salt;
- lemons;
- tea tree oil and, if you like the smell, lavender oil.

You can clean just about everything with that lot!

Whenever possible just use a microfibre cloth and water. E-Cloths are great, ninety-eight per cent of the dirt and bacteria will be wiped away. www.e-cloth. com.

Experiment for the best results. Often, I use a mix of water, distilled vinegar and a couple of drops of lavender oil and use the microfibre cloth, as it will clean surfaces, the loo, the bath or whatever. Tea tree oil will sort out any surfaces that need an antibacterial 'hit'.

Bathroom cleaning recipe:

There are hundreds of 'recipes' but my fave is probably my ultra-cheap bathroom cleaner. I use a half litre bottle (a reclaimed washing-up liquid bottle) and fill with:

1 ½ cups bicarbonate of soda mixed with 1 cup filtered or distilled water

2 tablespoons white vinegar or lemon juice

½ drop of essential oil

You can also add half a cup of liquid castile soap too. It works a treat!

Bicarbonate of soda

The major use of sodium bicarbonate is in foods such as baked goods. It is used in effervescent salts and is sometimes used medically to correct excess stomach acidity. The important thing is that it's environmentally friendly and cheap.

There's a wealth of uses for it apart from aiding digestion and here are just a few. Once you start using it, you'll start to discover your own uses.

- add bicarb to hot soapy dishwater. it will cut grease and speed removal of sticky foods on dishes and utensils

- after washing, soak your dishcloth in bicarb and water, swish out the sink and wring out the cloth; everything will be odour-free

- use as a non-abrasive cleaner for stainless steel sinks

- mix with borax (two tablespoons of each) and make your own dishwasher detergent (add a drop of lemon oil or fresh lemon if you want extra freshness)

- clean baby bottles with bicarb. nothing cleans plastic as well as bicarb, so make a paste and use with a sponge to scour plastic bowls. it won't scratch the surface

- fill vacuum flasks and teapots with a tablespoon of bicarb and water, let it stand then rinse thoroughly. it will stop teapots and coffee pots from staining and you can also remove tea stains from mugs by rubbing on a paste of bicarb and water

Here are some ideas to soak up smells:

(see also 'Air fresheners' below).

- keep an open box of bicarb in your fridge to avoid odours, bin it and start afresh every three months or so
- sprinkle bicarb in the bottom of your kitchen bin before you insert a fresh bin liner
- sprinkle bicarb inside smelly shoes (oh, come on, it can't just be me!) after wearing them and shake out excess powder the next morning; it will significantly reduce the whiff
- remove the smell of smoke from clothes by soaking in bicarb before washing

Bicarb is also useful when it comes to washing clothes. See 'Those washday blues' for more on that. Meanwhile there are, amazingly, even more uses for this wonder product. For instance, to clean jewellery, rub a paste of bicarb on to the piece, rinse off and buff dry.

Clean your oven with a paste of bicarb and 'elbow grease' or, to clean really dirty ovens, add distilled vinegar. Wash appliance exteriors with a mix of ¼ cup bicarb, ½ cup clear vinegar, 1 cup household ammonia and 1 gallon hot water. You can clean your windows with bicarb and you can also wipe down your venetian blinds with the stuff. Just about any surface can be cleaned with bicarb, even woodwork, and it can remove crayon marks from washable walls and linoleum floors.

> *Why do we love certain houses, and why do they seem to love us? It is the warmth of our individual hearts reflected in our surroundings.*
>
> T H ROBSJOHN-GIBBINGS

Remove wine or grease stains from a carpet by sprinkling the bicarb on immediately, dabbing up a little and leaving till the wine has been absorbed before vacuuming up any residue. Also, you can shake bicarb over carpets every few weeks and leave it for a while, overnight if possible, before vacuuming the next day.

There are hundreds more uses, but you get the idea. This wonderful, versatile little gem is available from good chemists. Get as big a box as you can for economy's sake. There are plenty of suppliers but you could try www.summernaturals.co.uk. They also sell borax (see below).

Soda crystals

Soda crystals are similar to bicarb but courser and with a granular texture but definitely not for internal use! Use soda crystals weekly to flush out drains. Dissolve some crystals in hot water and flush down to neutralise odours and get rid of blockages. You can also clean worktops, floors and greasy cookers and pans with soda crystals and water and, like bicarb, they work well as a solution mixed with white vinegar to clean teapots and chopping boards.

If I had a magic wand, I would ...

I wouldn't do anything differently because it's about continuing to learn, but I'd like the bigger picture to change towards a peaceful and more intelligently run world.

ROSI – TV STYLIST

Borax

Borax is a great old-fashioned 'powder' perfect for mixing with bicarb and excellent for laundry (not to be ingested though!).

It's always worth having plenty of household salt to mix with bicarb for many cleaning uses. Also, some recipes call for household ammonia. Just keep it out of the reach of kids!

Lemons and other natural solutions

No one ever dares throw away a lemon in my house. Even when it's wizened and long past its juicing days, it can be used for cleaning. Just a quick squirt will leave your sink or loo sparkling. Don't forget to slice off a bit of the rind and put that in the cutlery tray of the dishwasher for sparkly crockery but remember to remove it when you empty it or else it will be oh so soggy.

Nowadays, it's easy to find ecologically friendly products made from natural substances that are biodegradable. Ecover are the market leaders of eco cleaning, www.ecover.com. See also www.almawin.co.uk, www.livingclean.co.uk and www.seventhgeneration.co.uk.

If you have allergies, it's even more important to clean without chemicals and there are also many ways to help reduce allergens. Opt for a vacuum cleaner with a HEPA filter. You'll find lots of helpful tips at www.allergymatters.com. For non-allergenic bedding, ionisers and much more go to www.thehealthyhouse.co.uk.

Steam cleaners are wonderful for shifting stubborn dirt from surfaces, furnishings and even carpets but don't forget that, once you've loosened the dirt, the wet mess still has to be mopped up!

Dishwasher powder

Once you stop using too many chemicals around the home you'll really notice the terrible chlorine-type smell that seems to come from some of the commercial dishwasher tablets and liquid detergents. It's easy and cheap to make your own dishwasher powder and as long as you're scrupulous about scraping all the food off the dishes first and rinsing them it's just as effective as the shop bought ones and so much kinder to the environment.

Dishwasher recipe:

Take a large plastic container with a lid; mix 2 cups of borax and 2 cups of baking soda with half a cup of salt and half of citric acid (which you can get in chemists) and give it all a shake up. You can add a squeeze of lemon as you put it in the machine.

Personally, I find it hard to beat Ecover dishwasher tablets but if I run out I find you can just liberally sprinkle bicarbonate of soda across all the stacked crockery and add a bit of lemon rind to the cutlery tray – works a treat!

If I had a magic wand, I would ...

...pay all the Third World debts and help them use their resources. I would make all the sad children in the entire world happy.

MARIANO – MEDICAL DOCTOR, HERBALIST AND FOUNDER OF INLIGHT COSMETICS

Air fresheners

A recent study found that women and children – perhaps because they spend more time in the home environment – were particularly affected by headaches, insomnia and respiratory problems due to many bought air fresheners.

The chemicals contained in some of these products are known as VOCs (volatile organic compounds). They're low-level toxins that have been linked to a wide range of diseases and skin irritations.

So what are the alternatives? Well, air fresheners only mask a smell rather than attacking its source. So treat that first. Bicarbonate of soda is amazing for absorbing odours, as I mentioned earlier. Have you ever noticed that many of those 'shaky/powdery' types of fresheners contain vast quantities of bicarb anyway and are several times the price of raw bicarb? Why not cut out the middle man? Put some in a bowl and leave it next to smelly areas. Buy a big box. Don't bother with the tiny supermarket containers that are designed for cooking.

Plants are also wonderful for detoxing the home, absorbing vapours and releasing oxygen back into the atmosphere, thereby enhancing the air quality in your room. Remember those trailing spider plants we all had in the seventies that were very popular in student bedsits because they need zero care and attention? Research by NASA apparently found that just one spider plant can reduce dangerous levels of toxins in a room by over ninety per cent in twenty-four hours. They are also supposed to absorb the radiation from computers. Rubber plants are thought to be effective as well and, of course they're low-maintenance. They'll also survive with just a little bit of love and a wipe-down.

So, what if you want to introduce a nice fresh smell? There are a few ways. We all know the old trick of brewing fresh coffee and baking bread when we're trying to sell the house but lemons are also a fabulous, if rather expensive, way to get rid of any lingering odours. If you can get hold of them cheaply, simmer four lemons cut into quarters on the hob for around 45 minutes. Now there's a smell to give you a real kick.

If you want to whiz around with a spray (I know, there is something quite therapeutic about squirting something!), there's a very simple, very cheap alternative to chemical aerosols. Buy yourself a couple of plant spray bottles, at around £1.50 from any garden centre or bargain shop. Fill one with cold water and add two or three drops of essential oil. The choice is yours, depending on the smell you like but I usually keep one on the go that just contains tea tree oil, since it is a pretty effective room deodoriser as well as a wonderful, natural, mild antiseptic.

For another quick room deodoriser, soak a flannel or a cotton nappy in warm water, add a few drops of tea tree oil and place it over a radiator (do not put it over or even near a naked flame). Or you could fine-mist the area with an atomiser filled with 250ml hot water, 5 drops tea tree oil, and 5 drops lavender oil. Shake it well before use.

Stand a bowl of steaming water in your room (safely out of reach of children, of course!) and add 5–10 drops of tea tree oil, or use an aromatherapy lamp/candle. An electric diffuser is the safest – again, placed out of the reach of the kids.

Add a few drops of tea tree oil and lavender oil to a potpourri basket and place it on the floor under the radiator.

Back on topic, I keep another plant spray bottle on the go that has lavender oil and maybe a drop of geranium to lift my spirits. Other great ones are lemon oil and citronella, which both help scare off the wasps and mosquitoes in summer. Also, tea tree or eucalyptus with neroli is excellent if anyone in the family is coming down with a cold or flu.

I have a quick spray around once a day after cleaning or whenever a particular area needs it. Obviously, the water needs changing every few days. Even water with essential oils will start to whiff a little if left too long, as my husband so delicately pointed out when I forgot and used a bottle of lavender and water that had been kicking around for a couple of weeks – it smelled like a gents' urinal (well, only he would know!).

The spray will cost you in the region of £2 for a bottle and around £4 each for the oils and will last for ages.

If you do want to throw money at it and prefer a professional bottle on your shelf, you won't go wrong with the fabulous natural room sprays from www.spiezia organics.com, www.homescents.co.uk, www.lavera.co.uk.

If I had a magic wand, I would …

… make space to still my mind and gather my thoughts more often; make a conscious effort to just be 'in the moment' instead of rushing on to the next thing.

LYNDA – REFLEXOLOGIST
AND MUM OF THREE

Those washday blues

I've never liked using conventional detergents for laundry. I've tried using the non-biological liquid rather than powder but still find my skin feels dry and flaky. Also, if you care about the effect on the environment, here's a fantastic 'green' alternative that is very cost-effective, has no smells and works.

Balls

Yes, I'm talking balls, supercharged laundry balls, one of today's best-kept secrets! I'm astounded that more people don't know how brilliant these little wonders are. (I suspect the manufacturers don't have the marketing budgets that big detergent companies have.) Basically, they're little balls that are placed in the washing machine instead of regular detergent. They contain pellets, which produce ionised oxygen, activating the water molecules naturally, allowing them to penetrate deep into the clothing fibres to lift away the grime. They are totally environmentally friendly, unperfumed, non-toxic and very gentle to fabrics. Also, they are hypoallergenic and particularly suitable for babies and children, though you may have to remove the really stubborn stains from garments first. They also help to soften the water, so there is no need for fabric softener and, amazingly, they last for around a thousand washes, so they work out considerably cheaper than conventional detergents and are 'kinder' to the average washing machine. I'm a big fan and have been using them for about five years, and I don't stink (do I?). They can also be used for clothes that need hand-washing and often come with an eco friendly stain remover. www.ecozone.co.uk.

Remember, if you want a slight fragrance 'à la fabric softener', add one or two drops of lavender oil in the fabric softener compartment.

Guilty secrets and imperfections:

What a long list this could be!

If I had a magic wand, I would …

… eat less/drink less/do more exercise/have more fun with my children/shout less at my husband.

DINKA – FENG SHUI CONSULTANT,
MUM OF TWO

Nuts

We're talking soapnuts here. Their proper name is – wait for it – *Sapindus mukorossi* and they've been used to wash clothes and linen in India and Nepal forever.

They're not actually nuts but a berry. As they are not part of the nut family they won't cause any nut allergy (and they're a renewable resource). They grow as a cluster of berries, each containing a small, black seed. The outer bit of the berry, the fruit, is tough and leathery and full of saponin that acts like soap when it comes into contact with water.

For an average load of washing you need to add seven or eight half-shells to the drum with the clothes. Put them in a thin sock or a muslin bag. As with the laundry balls, they help to retain the colour and brightness of fabrics and there's no need for softener.

You can also make an infusion by boiling the nuts and straining off the liquid to use as a general cleaner. Soapnuts are one hundred per cent natural, so great for anyone with allergies and are totally environmentally friendly. They are also very economical at around £5 for a huge bag. www.ethicstrading.com, www.soapods.com, www.inasoapnutshell.com. Happy washing!

It goes without saying, of course, that, if you get an opportunity, wait for a nice day and hang your whites outside to dry. If they're yellowed or stained, squirt them with bit of lemon juice. It mixes beautifully with the sunshine and they come up like new.

It must be said that most of us don't fare well when it comes to aiming for an eco-friendly wash day. Of course, we should use a short wash cycle or economy programme and, to save money if you use a washing machine and tumble dryer most days, you'd do well to get your electricity priced on Economy 7, or your supplier's equivalent, because these appliances simply guzzle units of electricity, particularly tumble dryers. We've all been sold a bit of a pipe dream when it comes to these expensive items. Yes, they've got reverse action and we can get the clothes completely dry but at what cost to our pockets and our clothes? It's well documented that the majority of fabrics will last longer if they're not tumbled around in extreme heat and you'll have noticed that, if you put T-shirts and tops in there, after a few times the fabric starts to 'bobble'.

Guilty secrets and imperfections ...

Beer, chocolate, staying up too late, too much time on the computer and a lack of focus. Life is far too interesting to get trapped in one little rut.

CARL –

FOUNDER OF HEALTH CHAMPION

Top tip!

If you regularly need to dry your laundry quickly and want to save energy costs, get yourself an old-fashioned spin-dryer. Yes, the top-loading drum type that you will remember your mum had. In fact, if you ask her, your aunt or grandma now I bet they'll say, 'Oh, yes, my old spin-dryer was wonderful. I really don't know why I got rid of it.' Well, they got rid of it because washing machines offered high spin speeds and we were told tumble dryers were better but there is a world of difference. Even when the laundry has already been on a 1,400-spin cycle in the washing machine, first a trickle then a torrent of water will come gushing out of a spin dryer for about two minutes. Lo, almost completely dry laundry equivalent to over an hour in the tumble dryer at a fraction of the energy cost too!

Let's see if we can start a revival in old fashioned appliances. My mum says no way is she going back to her old mangle, though.

Clear your clutter

Out of clutter find simplicity. From discord find harmony. In the middle of difficulty lies opportunity.

ALBERT EINSTEIN

You know the deal – clutter takes over your life. The golden rule is if you haven't used something for six months and it's not especially beautiful to look at, get rid of it.

It's easier said than done and most of us have bulging wardrobes of clothes we'll never wear and cupboards stacked high with pans we'll never use. It's very responsible now to recycle your clothes, indeed everything you don't need and avoid buying new. When you really do need a new outfit organise a clothes swap party with friends or check out your local charity shop.

Try to team up with a friend regularly whose life also needs a 'declutter'. Let her loose in your wardrobe, basement or whatever and let her sort the piles. Someone else's perspective is fantastic and they won't get sidetracked by the old photos or be tempted to hold onto that dress that's two sizes too small just because you wore it on your first date. It's painful, but a sort of nice pain, and, boy, do you feel good afterwards!

I had the luxury of hiring a professional decluttering expert. Here are Naomi's top tips:

- clear one area at a time
- stay focused on the end result – reclaiming your space
- don't dither – if in doubt, chuck it out
- ask yourself if all this stuff makes you feel good
- put on your favourite music
- make separate piles (cherish, charity, chuck)
- do remember, you will always enjoy space more than stuff
- fill your life, not your home

Her book is *Simplify your Life – Downsize and De-stress* by Naomi Saunders (Sheldon Press). www.clearly organised.co.uk.

> *Have nothing in your home that you do not know to be useful and believe to be beautiful.*
>
> WILLIAM MORRIS

A wonderful website that's full of house-cleaning and organising is to be found at www.flylady.net. This hilarious American woman shares her daily routines and injects great humour into it all. As she says, 'If you're living in CHAOS (Can't Have Anyone Over Syndrome), it's time to do something about it.' If the whole idea still seems overwhelming, start with what she calls 'flying lessons', the 'fly lady's' very own suggestions for clearing clutter in a few easy steps. See also Organized Home at www.organizedhome.com.

A great way to recycle your unwanted items is to join www.freecycle.org.

Beat a retreat

If women were convinced that a day off or an hour of solitude was a reasonable ambition, they would find a way of attaining it. As it is, they feel so unjustified in their demand that they rarely make the attempt.

ANNE MORROW LINDBERGH

Girls, tell your fella that you're leaving! No, I'm not really advocating the break up of your marital (or otherwise) bliss, but I want to renew, refresh and invigorate it!

Experts say increasing numbers of women are suffering from a condition known as 'hurried woman syndrome'. It's caused by chronic stress from the demands of juggling work with a hectic family life. Sound like you?

I've certainly had an attack of it in the past but, as I write this, I'm sitting on the porch of a wonderful holistic B&B in Cornwall scribbling as fast as I can, no children, husband, work calls, domestic shenanigans – just me with a cup of organic Earl Grey and the low sun over the Cornish coast. It took me years to realise this, but you've got to get away! I call it beating a retreat.

It's only for a few days, I know, but that's enough! There simply isn't a machine, programme or drug that can lift your spirits like this. We all go through years of excuses, not having the time, the inclination, the

'I'm needed' syndrome: family needs me, husband needs me, work needs me and so it goes on. Yes, they need you but they need you happy, fresh, invigorated and full of life. One thing I do know is that graveyards are full of indispensable people. You've probably heard the one about the dying words that no one ever said 'I wish I had spent more time at the office'!

Now I go away on my own, just once every couple of years and DH (Darling Husband) is happy for me to do it. He can see just how much it benefits me and my whole outlook on many a thing.

So make yourself do it – guys too. Book a few days away, get the train somewhere, travel cheap, stay cheap. Be with yourself. It's amazing what you can sort out. You'll probably find yourself making a few life-changing decisions. There are a million and one locations. It could be a hotel in San Francisco, a beach hut in Whitstable or a convent on the Isle of Skye. Just escape! If you really are indispensable, just take an hour off and sit in a garden in silence. You'll find loads of ideas at www.thegoodretreatguide.com.

Life should not be a journey to the grave with the intention of arriving safely in an attractive, well preserved body, but rather to skid in sideways, chardonnay in one hand, strawberries in the other, body thoroughly used up, totally worn out, screaming 'woo …woo …what a ride!!!'

(IMPERFECT) AUTHOR UNKNOWN

Keep in touch

To contact Janey Lee Grace, email janey@imperfectly natural.com and check out www.imperfectlynatural. com for more tips, updates and info on forthcoming projects.